Introduction

TODAY'S WORLD OWES a great deal to the civilizations of ancient Europe. The Olympic Games, democratic government, Western ideas about law, poetry, drama and art all originated long ago in ancient Greece or Rome. Beautiful Greek temples such as the Parthenon in Athens, towering Roman aqueducts and long, straight Roman roads still survive from long ago. Modern languages such as English and especially French, Italian and Spanish are still peppered with words that come from Greek or Latin (the language of ancient Rome).

GREEK PERFECTION
The Parthenon in Athens represents the golden age of Greek civilization. Completed in 432BC, it was a temple to Athene, the goddess of wisdom. She was also patroness of farming and protector of the city.

PALACES AND WARRIORS

The story of European civilization begins in Crete, the largest of the Greek islands, where the "Minoan" culture developed from about 2000BC. The Minoan kings built magnificent palaces. Crete was well placed to profit from trade with ancient Egypt and with the even older civilizations of the Near and Middle East. It was from these regions that farming and metalworking skills had already entered Europe. Cretans of the Minoan age adopted methods of writing from Asia, creating the first scripts in Europe.

By 1600BC another culture was growing up on the Greek mainland, around rocky strongholds such as Mycenae. Mycenaean Greeks fought long wars with the city-state of Troy, which lay in what is now Turkey. Troy was finally sacked in about 1250BC. The heroic deeds of the warriors during and after the war were recorded about 500 years later, by a Greek poet called Homer.

A WOMAN'S PLACE
Caryatids were statues of women used to support the roofs of Greek temples. The name comes from the town of Caryae, whose citizens were reduced to slavery after supporting the Persian invasion of Greece.

SECRET INVASION
The blind poet Homer wrote about the siege of Troy in a long poem called *The Iliad*. Greek soldiers hid inside a huge wooden horse, which the Trojans dragged into the city of Troy. As night fell, the Greeks crept out and conquered the city.

TRADING STATES
The ancient land of Egypt traded with the first Greek civilization, on the island of Crete. Egypt was ruled by Greeks from 332 to 30BC and then by Romans until AD395.

GODS
and
GLADIATORS

PHILIP STEELE
RICHARD TAMES

southwater

This edition is published by Southwater

Southwater is an imprint of Anness Publishing Ltd
Hermes House, 88–89 Blackfriars Road
London SE1 8HA
tel. 020 7401 2077; fax 020 7633 9499
www.southwaterbooks.com; info@anness.com

UK agent: The Manning Partnership Ltd
tel. 01225 478444; fax 01225 478440;
sales@manning-partnership.co.uk

UK distributor: Grantham Book Services Ltd
tel. 01476 541080; fax 01476 541061;
orders@gbs.tbs-ltd.co.uk

North American agent/distributor:
National Book Network
tel. 301 459 3366; fax 301 429 5746;
www.nbnbooks.com

Australian agent/distributor: Pan Macmillan Australia
tel. 1300 135 113; fax 1300 135 103;
customer.service@macmillan.com.au

New Zealand agent/distributor: David Bateman Ltd
tel. (09) 415 7664; fax (09) 415 8892

Publisher: Joanna Lorenz
Editors: Joy Wotton and Elizabeth Woodland
Designers: John Jamieson, Stuart Watkinson at
Ideas Into Print
Jacket Designer: Sarah Williams
Illustration: Robert Ashby, Stuart Carter, Shane Marsh
Photography: John Freeman
Stylist: Thomasina Smith
Additional Styling: Melanie Williams
Prepress Controller: Neil McLaren
Production Controller: Darren Price

Anness Publishing would like to thank the following
children for modelling for this book: Mohammed Asfar,
Leon R. Banton, Afsana Begum, Lucilla Braune, Ha
Chu, Paula Dent, Frankie Timothy Junior Elliot, Aileen
Greiner, Rikky Charles Healey, Francesca Hill, Daniel
Ofori, Vanessa Ofori, Edward Parker, Eva
Rivera/Razbadavskite, Claudia Martins Silva, Clleon
Smith, Nicky Stafford, Simon Thexton, Shereen
Thomas, Ha Vinh, Saif Uddowlla and Kirsty Wells.
Gratitude also to their parents, and to Hampden
Gurney and Walnut Tree Walk Schools.

Previously published in two separate volumes, *Step Into
Ancient Greece* and *Step Into the Roman Empire*.

10 9 8 7 6 5 4 3 2 1

CONTENTS

THE GREEK WORLD

By 700BC Greek fortunes were reviving, after a long period of warfare and unrest. Greeks were sailing far and wide, founding new colonies on the shores of the Black Sea and on Mediterranean coasts, in North Africa, Italy, France and Spain. The Greeks were not united as a single nation or empire. Their city-states, such as Athens, Corinth or Sparta, were often at war with each other. Sometimes they joined together to fight a common enemy. In 479BC they fought off invasion by a huge army from Persia. This was the golden age of Greek civilization, a time of new political ideas, of philosophy, drama, art and architecture.

THE COLOSSAL COLOSSEUM
Rome's Flavian Amphitheatre, or Colosseum, staged bloodthirsty spectacles. Its arena had an area of 86 x 45m, and it could hold crowds of over 50,000.

CONQUEROR OF THE WORLD
Alexander the Great was one of the most successful soldiers the world has ever known. His empire stretched across the Middle East, Persia and Afghanistan.

THE AGE OF ALEXANDER

In 338BC the city-states were defeated by Philip II, ruler of a northern Greek kingdom called Macedonia. In 334BC his son and successor, a brilliant general called Alexander the Great, launched a united Greek invasion of Asia, creating an empire that stretched from Egypt to India. Following Alexander's early death in 323BC, rule of this empire was divided among his generals.

ROME TRIUMPHANT

A new power was now emerging in Europe. Rome had started life as a small village in Italy, in about 753BC. By 609BC the Romans had thrown off rule by kings to create a republic. By 250BC the Romans ruled all of Italy, and by 146BC they had conquered Greece itself. The Romans, ruled by emperors rather than people's representatives from 27BC, built up a vast new empire that stretched from Spain to Syria and from Britain to Egypt.

BUILDING BARRIERS
The Roman Empire's north-western frontier ran along Hadrian's Wall, which crossed the wild north of Britannia (Great Britain). Building began in AD122.

THE WOLF'S CHILDREN
A Roman myth tells how a wolf looked after Romulus and Remus, twin sons of the god Mars. As an adult, Romulus slew Remus and became Rome's first ruler.

A COMMON HERITAGE

One of the greatest Roman poets was Virgil, who lived from 70 to 19BC. He wrote a dramatic account of Rome's origins, claiming that the Romans were descended from warriors of Troy who had escaped from the city after it had been sacked by the Greeks, and then travelled until they came to Italy. This story was a complete invention, but it does tell us how the Romans always looked back to the Greek world for inspiration. Many Roman tutors and schoolmasters were Greeks, and educated Romans could speak and write in the Greek language. The gods and goddesses worshipped by the Romans were easily identifiable with those of ancient Greece. Roman Jupiter, father of the gods, was the same as Greek Zeus, while Venus, goddess of love, was the Greek Aphrodite. Alexander the Great was a hero to the Romans as well as the Greeks.

THE THINKING MAN
The Romans admired the ancient Greeks, and Greek philosophers, such as Socrates and Plato, influenced the way the Romans thought about things. Schoolchildren learned how to write in both Greek and Latin.

KING OF THE GODS
Jupiter, the sky god, was one of the most powerful of all the Roman gods. The Romans believed in many gods and goddesses, and some of them were the same as the gods of ancient Greece but with different names. Jupiter was called Zeus in ancient Greece.

SAY IT IN STONE
The Romans recorded all kinds of inscriptions in Latin on public buildings, temples and monuments. Their lettering influenced the way we print letters today.

AFTER THE FALL OF ROME

Rome remained the Western capital of the Roman empire until AD476, when the city fell to invading Germanic warriors. By then there was a separate Eastern capital of the empire, a city called Byzantium or Constantinople (modern Istanbul). This survived until 1453, when it was captured by Turks. Although the Byzantine Empire was founded by Romans, for most of its existence it was Greek in its customs and language. Rome itself remained very powerful during the Middle Ages as the headquarters of the Roman Catholic Church, whose language of worship remained Latin into modern times.

A GOOD DAY OUT
Like the ancient Greeks, the Romans enjoyed seeing plays and other entertainments in their open-air theatres. The largest theatre at Pompeii could seat up to 50,000 people.

PAST AND PRESENT

The story of both the Greeks and the Romans is a very exciting one, which can still thrill us today. It is full of extraordinary events and remarkable characters. Yet the more we learn about them, the more we realise that their everyday lives were very like our own. Dramatic proof of this comes from an Italian town called Pompeii. It was a very old settlement, and its inhabitants had included many peoples – Italians known as Etruscans and Samnites, also Greek colonial settlers.

By AD79 Pompeii was a typical Roman town, part of the mighty empire. That was the year in which Pompeii's streets were buried by ash from an erupting volcano called Vesuvius. The city disappeared and was lost. It was not until the 1700s that this lost world was rediscovered, and archaeologists have been uncovering it ever since. Their digging has revealed meals left on the table, kitchen pots and pans, graffiti on the streets, cosmetics jars and jewellery, fast food shops and bars, pet dogs and gardens. All these discoveries bring ancient history to life for us. They help us to step back in time.

MAKE IT CLASSICAL
In the 1700s and 1800s, Europeans were still inspired by ancient Rome. The Arc de Triomphe, designed in the Roman style, was built in Paris to commemorate the French victory at Austerlitz in 1805.

A NEW CITY
The city of Constantinople was named after the Roman emperor Constantine, who is shown on this gold coin. He reunited the Empire in AD324, and made Constantinople his imperial residence and the new capital in the East.

THE FALL OF THE ROMAN EMPIRE
From AD400 onwards, Rome was under constant attack from northern Europeans. Vandal warriors from Germany attacked the city of Rome in AD455, and the Western Empire finally fell in AD476.

BUILDING WITH STYLE
The fascination with all things Greek or Roman crossed the Atlantic Ocean to the New World. The Supreme Court of the United States moved into this classical building in 1935.

THE ANCIENT GREEKS

Greece, in south-eastern Europe, is a land of dusty plains and rugged mountains, baked brown in the heat of summer. It occupies the Balkan peninsula, whose ragged coastline breaks up into chains of islands across the deep blue waters of the Ionian and Aegean Seas. Scattered across both mainland and islands are the ruins of ancient temples, palaces, strongholds, battlefields and theatres. Here it is easy to be transported back in time, to imagine Spartan hoplites drilling for war, or athletes in training for the original Olympic Games. Welcome to Greece, a small country that changed the course of history thousands of years ago.

The World of the Ancient Greeks

STEP BACK IN TIME 3,000 YEARS to the shores of the eastern Mediterranean where one of the most enduring and influential civilizations of the Western world is emerging. Ancient Greece was made up of a number of self-supporting city-states, each of which developed a strong, individual identity. They developed from an agricultural society that wrote in simple pictograms into a sophisticated culture. Centuries on, the Greek legacy survives in parts of modern society. The origins of democracy, mathematics, medicine and philosophy can be traced back to this time in history. Even some of our words are made up from ancient Greek. "Telephone" comes from the ancient Greek words "tele" meaning far and "phonos" meaning sound.

A FEAT OF PERFECTION

The Parthenon is regarded as the supreme achievement of Greek architecture. It was the most important building in Athens, where it still sits on top of the Acropolis. The temple took 15 years to build and was dedicated to Athena, guardian goddess of Athens. Around 22,000 tonnes of marble, transported from over 15 km away, were used in its construction.

TIMELINE 6000BC–c.1100BC

The first people lived in Greece about 40,000 years ago. They were hunter-gatherers. Farming was not introduced until 6,000BC. The first great Greek civilization, and also the first in Europe, flourished on the island of Crete around 2000BC. This was the mighty Minoan civilization whose decline heralded in the glorious age of the Mycenaeans. After this a period known as the Dark Ages began. It was followed

a drinking vessel (rhyton) in the shape of a bull's head from Knossos

by the golden age of Classical Greece which lasted from about 500BC to 336BC.

*c.*6000BC The first settlers arrive on the island of Crete and the Greek mainland.

*c.*2900–1000BC The Bronze Age in Greece. People discover how to mix copper and tin to make bronze.

disc from Crete with unique pictographic script

*c.*2000BC Minoan civilization flourishes on Crete. The Minoans use a script called Linear A, which has not yet been deciphered.

*c.*1600BC The Mycenaeans dominate mainland Greece.

statuette of worshipping woman from Mycenae

40,000BC

6000BC

1600BC

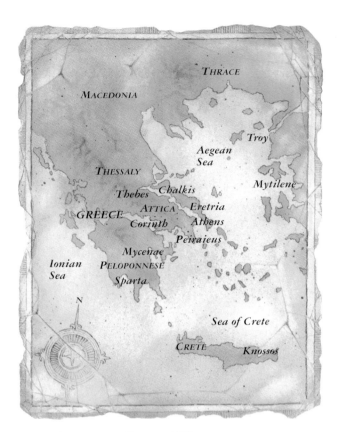

CENTRE STONE

The omphalos (navel) was a carved stone kept at the shrine at Delphi. The ancient Greeks thought that this holy sanctuary was the centre of the world. The omphalos stone was placed there to mark the centre. It was said to have been put there by Zeus, ruler of the gods. It may have also served as an altar on which sacrifices were made.

THE ANCIENT GREEK WORLD

The map above shows the main ports and cities through which the Greeks traded. The ancient Greek world centred on the Aegean Sea. The Greeks were adventurous seafarers. Trade took them from the Aegean Sea to the Atlantic Ocean and the shores of the Black Sea, where they formed many settlements. These colonies helped Greece to spread its influence beyond the mainland and its offshore islands.

THE PAST REVEALED

Archaeological evidence in the shape of pottery such as this vase help us to piece together the history of Greece. This vase is typical of the superior craftsmanship for which the Greeks were admired. It was common for vases to be decorated with pictures showing historical events. In this one, we see a scene from the siege of Troy in which the king is being murdered. The siege was an important event in Greek folklore. These decorative vases were used as containers for liquids such as oil, water and wine. The export of such pottery contributed an enormous amount of wealth to the Greek empire.

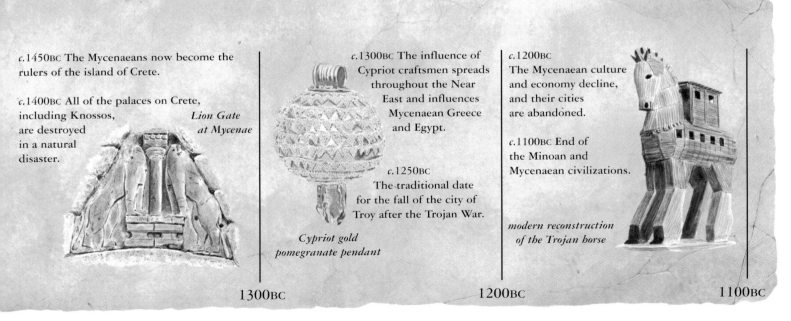

c.1450BC The Mycenaeans now become the rulers of the island of Crete.

c.1400BC All of the palaces on Crete, including Knossos, are destroyed in a natural disaster.

Lion Gate at Mycenae

c.1300BC The influence of Cypriot craftsmen spreads throughout the Near East and influences Mycenaean Greece and Egypt.

c.1250BC The traditional date for the fall of the city of Troy after the Trojan War.

Cypriot gold pomegranate pendant

c.1200BC The Mycenaean culture and economy decline, and their cities are abandoned.

c.1100BC End of the Minoan and Mycenaean civilizations.

modern reconstruction of the Trojan horse

1300BC 1200BC 1100BC

Power and Prosperity

THE HISTORY OF ANCIENT GREECE spans 20 centuries. It starts with the Minoan civilization on the island of Crete, which reached its height between 1900 and 1450BC. This culture was also the first to develop in Europe. The Minoans were a lively and artistic people who built palaces and towns and were also great seafarers. Their achievements greatly influenced the Mycenaeans, who built their own civilization on the Greek mainland from around 1600BC. Both the Minoan and Mycenaean cultures collapsed, probably under the impact of natural disasters and warfare, to be followed by centuries of poverty.

Revival was under way by 750BC and the Greek world reached its economic peak during the 5th century BC. This period is known as the Classical Age, when Athens was at the height of its power and prosperity. During this century, Athens led the Greeks into many victorious battles against Persia. However, Athens itself later suffered an economic decline because of a series of wars fought against its rival, Sparta. Then, in the 4th century BC, Greece was conquered by Macedonia. The Macedonian ruler Alexander the Great spread Greek culture throughout his empire. Finally, between 168 and 146BC Macedonia and Greece were absorbed into the Roman empire, and Greek civilization became part of the heritage that Rome passed on to the rest of Europe.

TRADE AND EXPANSION

The Classical Age in Greek history dates from around 500 to 336BC. This period was marked by an increase in the wealth of most Greek city-states. Greek trade ships were sailing throughout the Mediterranean and Black Sea. Colonies were also being set up on the shorelines of these two seas.

ITALY

• Locri

SICILY

• Naxos

• Syracuse

N

W

S

TIMELINE c.1100BC–400BC

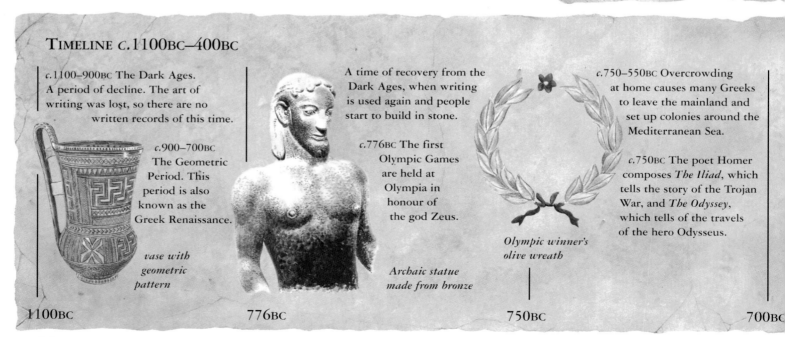

c.1100–900BC The Dark Ages. A period of decline. The art of writing was lost, so there are no written records of this time.

c.900–700BC The Geometric Period. This period is also known as the Greek Renaissance.

vase with geometric pattern

A time of recovery from the Dark Ages, when writing is used again and people start to build in stone.

c.776BC The first Olympic Games are held at Olympia in honour of the god Zeus.

Archaic statue made from bronze

Olympic winner's olive wreath

c.750–550BC Overcrowding at home causes many Greeks to leave the mainland and set up colonies around the Mediterranean Sea.

c.750BC The poet Homer composes *The Iliad*, which tells the story of the Trojan War, and *The Odyssey*, which tells of the travels of the hero Odysseus.

1100BC   776BC   750BC   700BC

MACEDONIA

Zeus

Black Sea

Trojan horse

Troy •

trireme

GREECE

ASIA MINOR

Aegean Sea

an Sea

• Thermopylae

• Delphi

• Thebes

Corinth

Parthenon

• Ephesus

discus thrower

Olympia

• Mycenae   Athens

Spartan warrior

• Sparta

Mediterranean Sea

CYPRUS

RHODES

Poseidon

Minotaur

CRETE

• Knossos

---

c.700–500BC The Archaic Period. During this period Greece expands. Athens becomes the largest and most influential of the independent city-states that make up Greece.

c.508BC Democracy is introduced in Athens. Every citizen has the right to speak and vote.

Odysseus gouges out the eye of a Cyclops

c.500–336BC The Classical Age. Greek culture and learning reaches its height.

c.480–479BC The Persian Wars. The Greeks are victorious, defeating the Persians at the battles of Marathon and Salamis.

Persian archer

c.479–431BC The golden age of Athens. Trade flourishes and the city grows very prosperous.

c.447–432BC The Parthenon is built in Athens.

the Parthenon

500BC

479BC

443BC

Famous Greeks

THE GREEKS TREASURED THEIR rich store of myths and legends about gods and heroes, but they also took a keen interest in human history. They valued fame and glory far more than riches. Their ultimate aim in life was to make a name for themselves that would live on long after death. Statues were put up in prominent places to honour Greeks who had won fame in different ways – as generals on the battlefield, as poets, teachers, philosophers, mathematicians, orators or sportsmen. These heroes represented the human qualities the Greeks most admired – physical courage, endurance and strength, and the intelligence to create, invent, explain and persuade.

HOMER (c700BC)
The blind poet Homer (above) was honoured for writing two epic tales. The first is *The Iliad*, a story about the siege of Troy. The other is *The Odyssey* which follows the adventures of Odysseus in his travels after the battle of Troy. Scholars now believe that the tales may have been written by two poets or even groups of several poets.

SAPPHO (c600BC)
The poet Sappho was born on the island of Lesbos. She wrote nine books of poetry, but only one complete poem survives. Beauty and love were the subjects of her poetry. Her work inspired other artists of the time and influenced many writers and poets in later centuries.

SOPHOCLES (496–406BC)
Only seven of Sophocles' plays have survived. He is thought to have written 123 altogether. Besides being a playwright, Sophocles was also a respected general and politician. His name means "famed for wisdom".

TIMELINE 440BC–140BC

443–429BC The great statesman, Pericles, dominates politics in Athens.

431–404BC The Peloponnesian Wars take place between Athens and its great rival, Sparta. The Spartans defeat the Athenians.

399BC The Athenian philosopher, Socrates is condemned to death because his views prove unpopular.

marble bust of the philosopher, Socrates

371BC Sparta is defeated by Thebes. Thebes becomes the leading power in Greece.

362BC Sparta and Athens combine forces to defeat the Thebans at the battle of Mantinea.

338BC The Greeks are defeated by the Macedonians at the battle of Chaeronea. Philip II of Macedonia becomes ruler of Greece.

iron corselet which is thought to have belonged to Philip II of Macedonia

336BC Philip II of Macedonia dies and is succeeded by his son, Alexander the Great. Alexander builds a huge empire, stretching from Greece as far east as India.

bronze statuette of Alexander the Great

443BC   371BC   336BC   334BC

PERICLES (495–429BC)

A popular figure and brilliant public speaker, Pericles was elected as a general 20 times. While in office, he built up a powerful navy and organized the building of strong defences, beautiful temples and fine monuments. He also gave ordinary citizens more say in government. Pericles' career ended after he led Athens into a disastrous war against Sparta. He was ostracized (expelled) as punishment for his misjudgement.

ALEXANDER THE GREAT (356–323BC)

Alexander was the son of Philip II of Macedonia. His life was spent in conquest of new territory, and his empire stretched across the Middle East, Persia and Afghanistan as far as the river Indus. His empire was swiftly divided when he died after suspected poisoning.

SOCRATES (469–399BC)

A renowned teacher and philosopher, Socrates encouraged people to think about how to live a good life. The Athenians sentenced him to die by drinking hemlock (a poison). Plato, Socrates' most brilliant pupil and himself a great philosopher, recorded his teacher's last days.

ARCHIMEDES (287–211BC)

The mathematician, scientist, astronomer and inventor, Archimedes came from Syracuse. When his city was besieged by the Romans, he designed a huge lens that focused sunlight on the Roman ships and set them on fire. He also devised a screw for raising water out of the ground and studied the concepts of floating and balance.

334BC Alexander the Great invades Persia to include it in his empire.

333BC The Persian army, led by King Darius, is defeated by Alexander the Great at the battle of Issus.

331BC Alexander the Great becomes king of Persia after defeating the Persians at the battle of Gaugamela.

King Darius of Persia

Romulus and Remus, legendary founders of Rome

323BC Alexander the Great dies, and his successors fight over the throne.

275BC Greek colonies are taken over by the Romans.

168BC Rome defeats the Macedonian rulers of Greece.

147–146BC The Achaean War. The Romans take control of Greece and Macedonia.

Roman soldier in full armour

323BC   196BC   146BC

The Minoans

A T THE HEART OF THE MINOAN CIVILIZATION was a huge palace at Knossos. The palace was a great political and cultural centre, and it controlled much of central Crete. At the height of its prosperity around 2000BC, over 10,000 people lived in the palace. Despite its obvious wealth, the palace was left unfortified because its rulers believed that their fleet could overcome any invaders. However, around 1450BC, the warlike Mycenaean Greeks captured Knossos and destroyed all the other Minoan palaces and towns.

In the early 1900s, British archaeologist Sir Arthur Evans unearthed the splendid remains of an ancient civilization on the island of Crete. He named it "Minoan" after the legendary Cretan king Minos, son of Zeus. It was discovered that the Minoans did not speak Greek and their writing, known as Linear A, has still not been decoded.

PURPOSEFUL POT
This brightly decorated pot from Knossos was probably used to hold water or wine. Sir Arthur Evans used the changes in pottery style to work out a chronology of the Minoan civilization. This pot was made around 1700–1550BC, on a potter's wheel.

A SPECIAL OCCASION
Frescoes were a popular art form used to decorate the walls of Cretan palaces. In order to make them last, frescoes were painted straight on to the wet plaster walls. This fresco shows a group of women gathered to watch a show or ceremony. Brightly coloured outfits with tight bodices and flounced skirts, as worn by the women here, were typical of the period.

MINOAN SEAL
You will need: work board, white and brown self-drying modelling clay, rolling pin, modelling tool, ruler, needle, PVA glue, water, mixing bowl, paintbrush, soft cord.

1 Roll out a small piece of white self drying modelling clay until it is about 1cm thick. Using a modelling tool, cut a small circle 3cm in diameter.

2 With the modelling tool carve the pattern shown above into the white clay. Leave to dry. This piece is the mould for the seal.

3 Roll a piece of the brown clay into a circle 2cm thick, and 3·5cm in diameter. Gently press the mould into the clay to leave an imprint.

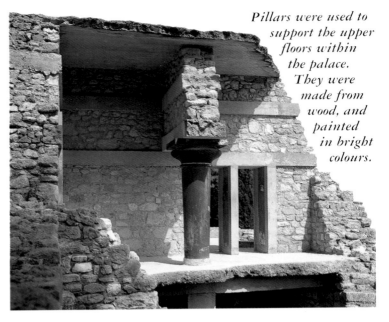

Pillars were used to support the upper floors within the palace. They were made from wood, and painted in bright colours.

LIVING IN LUXURY

The queen had her own set of apartments in the magnificent palace at Knossos. A large fresco decorates the wall in this room. It shows lively dolphins and fish swimming underwater. Most Minoan frescoes show scenes from palace life and the natural world. The paintings are a vital source of information for modern historians.

PALACE COMPLEX

The ruins of the great palace complex at Knossos have been excavated and partially reconstructed. Many of the Cretan palaces seem to have expanded with the random addition of rooms and corridors. Knossos was the largest of these palaces.

ROYAL SYMBOL

The double-headed axe was an important symbol in Minoan religion. This one was made from gold in about 1800BC.

A DANGEROUS DANCE

Bull-leaping was a popular form of entertainment in Crete. Both men and women took part in the sport. The young person would somersault over a charging bull's horns and then leap off its back. This sport may have been part of a religious rite.

4 Cut around the imprint leaving an edge 1cm wide. Make 2 small holes on each side of the circle with the needle. Leave to dry. This piece is the seal.

5 Prepare the varnish by mixing 2 parts of glue to 1 part of water. Brush the seal with varnish. Make sure that the holes aren't filled in with it.

6 Leave the varnish to dry. Cut a length of cord and thread it through either one or both holes. Wear it on your wrist or around your neck.

Seals were used as an identity badge, as a sign of ownership, as a lucky charm or as a piece of art.

17

The Mycenaeans

FRUIT OF LABOUR
This gold pomegranate pendant was found in a tomb on the island of Cyprus. The surface is decorated with fine grains of gold using a process known as the granulation technique. It took a skilled artist to make such a detailed piece of jewellery.

THE FIRST IMPORTANT CIVILIZATION on mainland Greece developed in the north-eastern part of the Peloponnese between 1600 and 1200BC. A series of small kingdoms and great fortresses were built during this period. The most powerful of these kingdoms was Mycenae. The Mycenaeans did not keep historical records, and therefore our knowledge of them comes largely from archaelogical evidence. We know that they were an advanced culture as they communicated in a written language and developed technology.

The Mycenaeans had the ability to quarry and build. Excavations have revealed high walls made from huge stone slabs. They learnt how to sail ships and developed extensive trade routes to Egypt, the Near East and the Baltic Sea. From these distant shores they imported gold, tin to make bronze, and amber for jewellery. Local resources such as olive trees were exploited for large financial gain. Oil was extracted from the olives, then perfumed and bottled for export.

Around 1200BC the Mycenaean culture suffered an economic recession that led to its downfall. Historians believe that earthquakes, wars and fires may have triggered the recession.

BOAR HELMET
The Mycenaeans favoured elaborate armour, such as this 13th-century BC helmet plated with boar's tusks. Other materials used to make armour included linen, leather and bronze. A great deal of weaponry has been excavated from the royal shaft graves at Mycenae.

COPYCAT CUTTLEFISH
The Mycenaeans developed many of their ideas from those of the Minoans who lived on the island of Crete. Cuttlefish designs similar to the one shown here are also found on Minoan pottery. Mycenaean pottery was widely traded and has been found as far away as northern Italy and eastern Spain. Small jars for holding perfumed olive oil were among the most popular wares.

DECORATED DAGGER

This inlaid bronze dagger came from the tomb of a wealthy Mycenaean who was buried between 1550 and 1500BC. The large number of weapons placed in the tombs of high-ranking individuals suggests that the Mycenaeans were a warlike people. Several such daggers have been discovered during excavations. This one is the most well preserved of them. The scene on the blade of the dagger shows leopards hunting in the forest. The illustration was built-up with inlays of different metals, including gold, silver and copper.

This dagger is the only one discovered with its golden hilt still attached.

MASKED MONARCH

Gold death masks like this are unique to Mycenae. They were made by beating a sheet of gold over a wooden mould, which had been carved in the image of the deceased. The mask was then laid over the face of the dead man when he was buried. This one was discovered by the archaeologist Heinrich Schliemann in the 1870s, after his excavation of Troy. In the past, people have incorrectly thought that the mask belonged to the heroic King Agamemnon. In fact, the mask is approximately three centuries older than first thought and dates from around 1500BC. It is now believed to be the death mask of one the earliest kings of Mycenae.

RICHES FROM GRAVES

Heinrich Schliemann's excavations at Mycenae in 1876 led to the uncovering of five royal shaft graves. They contained 16 bodies and rich treasures made of gold, silver, ivory and bronze. The contents of the graves prove that the Mycenaeans were a wealthy civilization. Important tombs were hollowed out of soft rock or built of stone. Ordinary people were buried in stone-slab coffins or simple pits.

Politics and Government

THE GREEK WORLD WAS MADE UP of about 300 separate city-states. Some were no bigger than villages, while others centred around cities such as Sparta or Athens. Each city-state was known as a *polis* (from which we take our word politics) and had its own laws and government. In the 4th century BC, the Greek philosopher, Aristotle, wrote that there were three types of government. The first was power held by one person. They could either be a king (who ruled on account of his royal birth), or a tyrant (who ruled by force). The second type was government by the few which meant rule by an aristocracy (governing by right of noble birth) or an oligarchy (a ruling group of rich and powerful men). The third type was a democratic government (rule by the many) which gave every male citizen the right to vote, hold public office or serve on a jury. Democracy was only practised in Athens. Even there women, slaves and foreigners were not counted as full citizens.

SET IN STONE
The laws of the city of Ephesus were carved on stone tablets in both Greek and Latin. The Greeks believed that their laws had to be clearly fixed (set in stone) and seen by everyone if all citizens were expected to obey them.

BEHIND THE SCENES
Women were not allowed to take an active part in politics in ancient Greece. However, some played an important role behind the scenes. One such woman was Aspasia. As a professional entertainer, she met and became mistress to Pericles (one of the most influential Athenian statesmen of the 5th century BC). Pericles confided in his mistress about affairs of state, and he came to rely on her insight and wisdom in his judgement of people and situations.

VOTING TOKENS
You will need: pair of compasses, thin card, pencil, ruler, scissors, rolling pin, cutting board, self-hardening clay, modelling tool, balsa wood stick 5cm long, piece of drinking straw 5cm long, bronze-coloured paint, paintbrush, water pot.

1 Make two templates. Use a pair of compasses to draw two circles, on a piece of thin card. Make each one 4cm in diameter. Cut them out.

2 Use a rolling pin to roll out the clay to 3cm thickness. Use a modelling tool to cut around the card circles into the clay. Press down hard as you do this.

3 Make a hole in the centre of each clay circle. Use the balsa wood to make one hole (innocent token). Use the straw to make the other hole (guilty token).

PEOPLE POWER

Solon the Lawgiver was an Athenian statesman and poet who lived from 640 to 559BC. Around 594BC, when serving as chief magistrate, he gave Athens new laws that enabled more people to take part in politics. His actions prevented a potential civil war between the few nobles in power and the people who suffered under their rule.

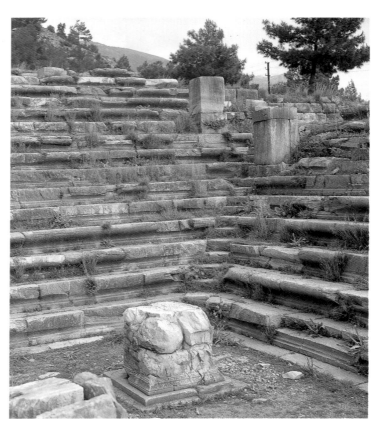

VOTE HERE

This terracotta urn was used to collect voting tokens. They were used in Athens when votes needed to be taken in law courts or when the voters' intentions needed to be kept secret. Each voter put a bronze disc in the urn to register his decision. Normally, voting was done by a show of hands, which was difficult to count precisely.

FACE TO FACE

The ruins of this council chamber at Priene in present-day Turkey show how seating was arranged. The tiered, three-sided square enabled each councillor to see and hear clearly all of the speakers involved in a debate. Even in the democracies of ancient Greece, most everyday decisions were taken by committees or councils and not by the assembly of voters.

4 Write a name on the innocent token using the modelling tool. Carefully push the balsa stick through the hole. Leave it to dry.

5 Write another name on the guilty token using the modelling tool. Carefully push the drinking straw through the hole. Leave it to dry.

6 Wait until the clay tokens are dry before painting them. The original tokens were made from bronze, so use a bronze-coloured paint.

Jurors were issued with two tokens to vote with. A hollow centre meant that the juror thought the accused was guilty. A solid centre meant that the juror thought the accused was innocent.

Equality and Inequality

Greek society was divided by a strict social structure, enforced by its governments. Most city-states were ruled by a small group of people (*oligarchy*). Two exceptions to this rule were the powerful cities of Sparta and Athens. Sparta held on to its monarchy, while Athens introduced the first democratic government in history. In the city of Athens, all citizens could vote and hold office. However to be a citizen, it was necessary to be an adult male, born in the city itself. Even so-called democratic Athens was ruled by a minority of the people who lived there. The treatment of women, foreign residents (called *metics*), slaves and children was just the same as in other city-states.

Women had no legal rights and rarely took part in public life. Metics were obliged to pay extra taxes and serve in the military. They could not own land or marry an Athenian. The Athenians felt uneasy about the large number of metics living in their city, but their skills helped to make it rich. Slaves made up half the population of Athens. Most had either been born slaves or become slaves as prisoners of war or captives of pirates. Even native Greeks could become slaves by falling into debt, but they were freed once the debt was paid off.

Warriors and Wealth

Only the most wealthy members of society could afford to equip themselves for war as fully armed infantrymen. In earlier centuries the poor were given supporting jobs, such as slinger or carrier of supplies. They could not afford expensive bronze weapons. However, as cities grew richer, weapons were manufactured at public expense by slaves, and most male citizens were expected to carry arms.

A Woman's Place

Greek women spent their lives at home. On this vase, made about 450BC, a woman ties her sandal before going out. As she has attendants, she must be wealthy. Poor women would leave the house to fetch water, work in the fields or shop in the market. Women with slaves, like this one, might leave the home to visit relatives or to pray at a shrine or temple.

Loved Ones

A young girl and her pet dog are seen on this tombstone from the 4th century BC. The likely expense of such a detailed carving suggests that she was dearly loved. Not all children were cherished. Girl babies, and sick babies of either sex, were often left outside to die. Some were underfed and fell victim to diseases. Greek law required children to support their parents in old age, so childless couples were always keen to adopt and were known to rescue abandoned children.

CRAFTSMAN

This smith could be a slave working in a factory owned by a wealthy man. Most craftsmen were slaves, ex-slaves, or foreign residents (*metics*). They were looked down upon by other citizens. If a master owned a talented slave, he might set the slave up to run his own business. In return, the master would receive a share of the profits. This smith might also have been a free, self-employed man, with his own workshop and a slave or two working as his assistants.

PATH TO POWER?

Being able to read and write in ancient Greece was not an automatic key to success. The Greek alphabet could be learned quite easily. Even slaves could become highly educated scribes. However, illiterate men were unlikely to hold high positions, except perhaps in Sparta, where written records were rarely kept. Although women were denied the right to a formal education, they were often able to read and write enough to keep a record of household stores.

ENSLAVED BY LANGUAGE

This Roman bottle is made in the shape of an African slave girl's head. The Greeks also owned slaves. The Greek philosopher Aristotle argued that some people were "naturally" meant to be slaves. His opinion was shared by many of his countrymen. He felt that this applied most obviously to people who did not speak Greek. Slaves were treated with varying degrees of kindness and hostility. Some were worked to death by their owners, but others had good jobs as clerks or bailiffs. A few hundred slaves were owned by the city of Athens and served as policemen, coin-inspectors and clerks of the court.

The Golden Age of Athens

ATHENS WAS THE CHIEF CITY of the fertile region of Attica, in southern Greece. It grew rich from trade, manufacturing and mining silver. The city of Athens reached the height of its wealth and power in the 5th century BC. By this time, it had built up a large empire which encompassed cities on both the mainland and the islands. Its 250,000 citizens enjoyed a vibrant golden age of art and culture. During this period, the Athenians celebrated a victory against Persian invaders by building a series of magnificent temples on the Acropolis in Athens. The Acropolis was a sacred hill that overlooked the city. Its most important temple was the Parthenon, which was dedicated to the city's goddess, Athena. Below, at the heart of the city was the market-place (*agora*). Surrounded by temples and public buildings and crowded with stalls, the agora was the commercial centre of Athens.

Between 431 and 404BC, Athens fought a crippling war against Sparta and the Persians. It lost the war and most of its maritime empire. As a result, Athens gave up its role as commercial and cultural leader in Greece to Sparta.

GODDESS OF WAR
On this 4th-century BC coin, Athena is shown wearing a helmet. It is wreathed with the laurel leaves of victory. Athena represented the disciplined side of fighting and was thought to have invented ships and chariots. As the goddess of war, she was known as Athena Nike, which means "Victory". Her counterpart was the god Ares who represented the madness and waste of war.

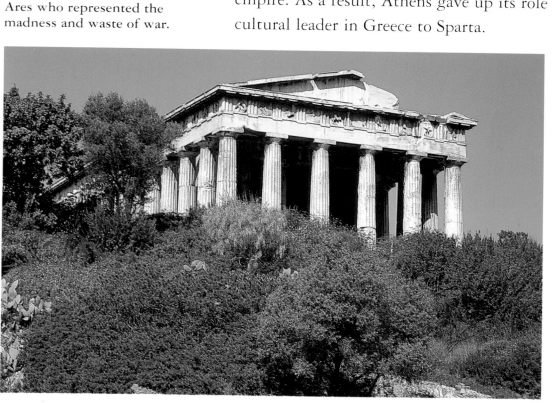

CROWNING GLORY
This temple to Hephaestus is a supreme example of the elegant architecture at which the Athenians excelled. It was built between 449 and 444BC at the eastern end of the agora. Hephaestus was the god of fire and armourer of the gods. A bronze statue inside the temple showed Hephaestus at work making armour, wearing a blacksmith's cap and holding a hammer above an anvil. Excavations have revealed that the bronze sculptors worked on one side of the temple, while sculptors in marble worked on the other side.

PANATHENAIC FESTIVAL

Every year, the people of Athens marched or rode in a great procession up to Athena's temple on the Acropolis. Even foreign residents joined in. This frieze from the Parthenon shows young men getting ready to join the procession. At the temple, oxen and other animals were sacrificed, and the meat was given to the people to eat. Every fourth year, there was an extra celebration when a new robe (*peplos*) was presented to the goddess Athena. This event was celebrated with days of sporting and musical competitions, with prizes of money or olive oil.

BIRTH OF A GODDESS

According to Greek legend, Zeus swallowed a pregnant lover after a prophecy warned that their child would depose him. Not long after swallowing her, Zeus complained of a painful headache. Hephaestus offered to split open Zeus's head with an axe to ease the pain. When he did, the goddess Athena jumped out. She was fully grown and wearing the armour of a warrior (as seen here in the centre of the painting).

BANISHMENT

Once a year, Athenians were allowed to banish an unpopular member of the community from the city for 10 years. Voters scratched the names on a fragment of pottery called an ostrakon, which is why the procedure was called ostracism. If at least 6,000 votes were cast in favour of exiling a person, they would have to leave the city within 10 days. Ostraka were also used for messages and shopping lists.

GODDESS OF WISDOM

The owl, symbolizing wisdom, was the emblem of Athena. This silver coin was issued in Athens in 479BC, after the Greeks won decisive victories against the Persians. Athenian coins were accepted throughout Greece, Italy and Turkey. This proves just how influential the city of Athens. Coins from other city-states were not widely accepted.

The Spartan Order

HEROIC KING
This bust from the 5th century BC may be of King Leonidas. There were two royal familes in Sparta. A king was chosen from each family to govern Sparta at the same time. Their powers were limited. Their main responsibility was to lead Spartan forces into battle.

AT THE HEIGHT OF ITS POWER, Sparta was the only city-state to rival the influence of Athens. It controlled most of the area of southern Greece, called the Peloponnese. Sparta was an insular and militaristic state. It became so after losing control of its slave population in a rebellion, which lasted for 17 years. The slaves (helots) were descendants of the people of Messenia whom Sparta overran in the 8th century BC. The helots outnumbered their Spartan overlords by seven to one. Although the Spartans defeated the rebellion, they continued to live in fear of another one. As a result, all male citizens were required by law to serve as full-time warriors. In addition, harsh restrictions were placed on the helots who were forbidden to ride horses or stay out after nightfall. While the citizens were fully occupied with military training, the heavy work and domestic chores were done by the helots.

The Spartans imposed strict living conditions on themselves. Spartan boys and girls were separated from their parents and brought up in barracks. Boys were trained for battle from the age of seven. They were kept cold, barefoot and hungry, and regularly flogged to make them tough. At the age of 20 they joined a group of 15 men who became their comrades. In Sparta, comradeship between men was more important than family life. The girls also took part in physical training so as to be able to bear healthy children. The power of Sparta declined after its defeat by the Theban army in 371BC.

WINE FOR THE WARRIORS

This massive bronze krater (wine vessel) stands 165 cm high, weighs 208 kg and holds 1,200 l of liquid. It was made around 530BC by a Spartan craftsman. The neck of the krater is decorated with Spartan warriors and chariots marching to war. The handles are crafted with the heads of female monsters called gorgons. It is thought that the vase was presented as a gift to the king of Lydia who wanted to form an alliance with Sparta. The Spartans were admired for the high quality of their bronze work.

DEATH AND GLORY

This modern monument was erected to commemorate the heroic self-sacrifice of King Leonidas and 300 Spartans. They died in 480BC defending the pass at Thermopylae against a Persian army 250,000 strong. The pass was just 13 m wide and the Spartans held their ground for two days while waiting for reinforcements. On the third day, a traitor showed the invading Persians another way through the mountain. Leonidas ordered a retreat, then led the rearguard in a fight to the death.

SEA POWER

The ivory relief pictured here has a Spartan warship carved into it. The pointed ram at the front was used for sinking enemy ships. Sparta was first and foremost a land power. Its navy was no match for that of Athens. A navy was expensive to run because specialized warships could not be used in peace-time. The Athenians financed their navy from their silver mines, but the Spartans were not so wealthy. They sometimes had to borrow money to keep their navy afloat.

BACKBONE OF THE ARMY

Spartan soldiers were easily distinguished on the battlefield because of their long hair and bright red cloaks. This figurine of a Spartan warrior probably dates from the 6th century BC. His crested helmet incorporates a nose guard and cheek guards. He is also wearing greaves (armour to guard his lower legs) and a cuirass (armour to protect his chest).

LAW-GIVER

This Roman mosaic probably shows the figure of Lycurgus, wielding an axe. Little is known of his life, because so few records were kept in Sparta. It is generally believed that Lycurgus lived around 650BC. His main achievement was to re-organize the government of Sparta for effective warfare after its disastrous defeat by the state of Argos.

the roof was made of pottery tiles

At Home

Greek homes were built of mud bricks and roofed with pottery tiles. They had small high windows with wooden shutters to keep out thieves, and floors of beaten earth, plaster or mosaic. Most houses started as small structures, and more rooms were added as the owner could afford them. This gave homes a random appearance and meant that streets were rarely straight. In country areas, houses were often surrounded by a stone wall to protect the inhabitants and their domestic animals. Men and women lived in separate rooms and in different areas of the house. The women's quarters were usually found at the rear of the house. Richer households might also have rooms for cooking and bathing in. Most homes contained only a few pieces of plain furniture which might include couches that doubled as beds, chairs and tables. Only wealthier people could afford richly decorated furniture such as couches inlaid with gold and ivory.

the andron was the room in which men entertained

the mosaic floor was made from brightly coloured pebbles

HOME HEATING
In mountainous areas of Greece, the winter can be very cold. This bronze brazier, dating from the 4th century BC, would have been filled with charcoal and used to heat a chilly room.

HEARTH GODDESS
Hestia was the goddess of the hearth and home. A fire was kept burning in her honour all year round. This fire was used for cooking, for heating water and to make charcoal as fuel for the braziers. Traditionally, when the Greeks founded a colony overseas, they took with them fire from their old home to link the new with the old.

DOLPHIN FRESCO
You will need: pencil, sheet of white paper 21cm x 19cm, rolling pin, white self-hardening clay, ruler, cutting board, modelling tool, pin, sandpaper, paintbrush, acrylic paints, water.

1 Draw a dolphin on the piece of white paper. Add some smaller fish and some seaweed. Refer to the final picture as a guide for your drawing.

2 Roll out a piece of clay until it measures 21cm across and 19cm down. The clay should be about 0.5cm thick. Cut off any uneven edges.

3 While the clay is still damp, place the dolphin picture over it. Following the outline of your picture, prick holes through the paper on to the clay.

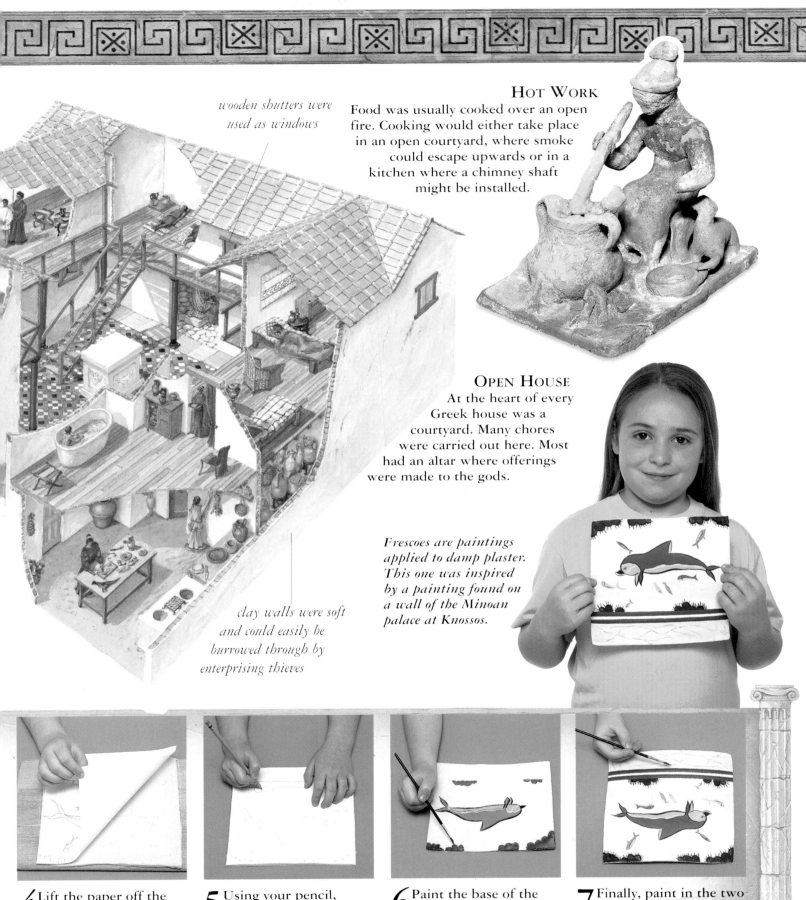

wooden shutters were used as windows

HOT WORK

Food was usually cooked over an open fire. Cooking would either take place in an open courtyard, where smoke could escape upwards or in a kitchen where a chimney shaft might be installed.

OPEN HOUSE

At the heart of every Greek house was a courtyard. Many chores were carried out here. Most had an altar where offerings were made to the gods.

Frescoes are paintings applied to damp plaster. This one was inspired by a painting found on a wall of the Minoan palace at Knossos.

clay walls were soft and could easily be burrowed through by enterprising thieves

4 Lift the paper off the clay and leave the base to dry. Once the clay has dried completely, sand it down with fine sandpaper for a smooth finish.

5 Using your pencil, join the dots of each outline together. When this is complete you will have a replica of your original drawing.

6 Paint the base of the fresco with a light blue. Once this is dry, paint in the rest of the picture. Use colours that reflect those of the sea.

7 Finally, paint in the two stripes at the bottom of the picture. These indicate where the fresco would have ended on the wall. Leave to dry.

Country Living

MOST GREEKS LIVED IN the countryside and worked as farmers. The mountainous landscape, poor, stony soil and hot, dry climate restricted what crops they could produce and which animals they could keep. Olive trees and bees flourished in these conditions. Olives provided oil and bees supplied honey (the main sweetener in food) and wax. Grain, such as barley, was difficult to grow, and the land used for its production had to be left fallow every other year to recover its fertility. Country people kept oxen to pull ploughs and drag heavy loads, and they used donkeys to carry goods to market. Rural areas also produced important materials used by city craftworkers. These included timber, flax for linen, horn and bone for glue, and leather.

Country life was hazardous, as droughts, floods, wolves and warfare threatened their livelihoods. Over the centuries, another problem developed. As forests were cut down for timber and fuel, soil erosion increased, leaving even less fertile land. The search for new agricultural land prompted the growth of Greek colonies along the shores of the Mediterranean and the Black Sea.

OLIVE HARVEST
This vase shows men shaking and beating the branches of an olive tree to bring down its fruit. Olives were eaten and also crushed to extract their oil. The oil was used for cooking, cleaning, as a medicine and a fuel for lamps.

FOOD FOR THE POT
Meat was obtained through hunting and the rearing of domesticated animals. Hunting was considered a sport for the rich, but it was a serious business for the poor, who hoped to put extra food on their tables. Simple snares, nets and slings were used to trap lizards and hares and to bring down small birds.

GONE FISHING
Many Greeks lived near water. The sea, rivers and lakes provided fish and shellfish which were their main source of protein. Fish was smoked or salted for future use. Always at the mercy of storms and shipwreck, fishermen prayed to the sea god Poseidon to save them.

PLOUGHING WITH OXEN

This terracotta figure from Thebes shows a farmer ploughing with two oxen. The plough was made of wood, but the part that broke up the earth was tipped with iron. Oxen were stronger and less expensive than horses, making them ideal for heavy work. When oxen died, they yielded hides for leather as well as horn, meat, sinew, which was used as twine, and fat that could be turned into candle tallow.

HARVEST GODDESS

Demeter was the goddess of grain and growth. She looked after plants, children and young people. The first part of her name *deme* is an ancient word for the Earth, the second part, *meter*, means "mother". Farmers believed that their success depended on uncontrollable forces such as the rain, the Sun, and diseases which attacked plants and livestock. Special prayers and sacrifices were made to Demeter to ask for her help in preventing such disasters. Festivals were held in honour of the goddess at crucial times during the harvest, before ploughing, when the corn began to sprout, and after it had been harvested.

SNACKS

Drying food was a good way of preserving it in a warm country like Greece. The Greeks ate raisins and dried apricots as a dessert or used them to sweeten other foods. Olives were another popular snack or appetizer.

olives

apricots

raisins

31

Food and Drink

MEALS IN ANCIENT GREECE were based around home-baked bread, fish fresh from the sea and such vegetables as onions, beans, lentils, leeks and radishes. Chickens and pigeons were kept for their eggs and meat, and a cow or a few goats or sheep for milk and cheese. Occasionally a pig or goat was slaughtered for the table, or hunting provided boar, deer, hares and even thrushes. The Greeks cooked their meat in olive oil and flavoured it with garlic and wild herbs. They ate fruits such as figs, apples, pears and pomegranates, which could be dried for the winter months. During hard times, people resorted to eating wild berries, hedgehogs and even locusts. Wine was the Greeks' favourite drink. It was usually very thick and had to be strained and then diluted with water for drinking. Sometimes it was mixed with resin, a preservative extracted from pine trees. It could then be kept for three to four years.

WASTE CONVERTER
This terracotta figure shows a butcher killing a pig. Pigs were a cheap source of meat because they could be kept on scrubby pasture and fed on acorns and kitchen scraps. Their skins were tanned to make leather and their hooves melted to make glue.

STORAGE ON A GRAND SCALE
Huge storage jars were used by the Greeks to store food and drink. These come from the palace, at Knossos in Crete. They probably contained olive oil, wine and cereals and were capable of holding hundreds of litres. Handmade from clay, they kept food and drink cool in the hot Mediterranean climate.

PANCAKES WITH HONEY AND SESAME SEEDS
You will need: 100g flour, sieve, mixing bowl, fork, 200ml water, 8 tablespoons clear honey, frying pan, 1 tablespoon sesame seeds, spoon, 1 tablespoon oil, spatula.

1 First make the pancake mix. Sieve the flour into a mixing bowl. Then, using a fork stir the water into the flour. Measure the honey into a small bowl.

2 Spoon the honey into the pancake mixture a bit at a time. Mix it with a fork, making sure that there are no lumps in the pancake mixture.

3 Ask an adult to help you with the next two steps. Heat the frying pan. Sprinkle in the sesame seeds and cook until browned. Set aside.

STAFF OF LIFE
A team of bakers prepare bread for the oven in this terracotta model. In big cities, commercial bakeries produced many different kinds of bread. Ordinary loaves were made of barley or wheat flour, speciality breads were flavoured with mountainside herbs, and delicious pastries came drenched in honey.

PLAY THE GAME
The Greeks drank from large, shallow cups such as this one. This picture shows a man playing a drinking game called *kottabos*. After much drinking, guests would compete to see who was most in control of their faculties by throwing the wine left in the bottom of their cup at a target. In another game, guests tried to make the loudest noise with their cup without spilling its contents.

GOD OF WINE
This Roman stone panel shows a procession of revellers following the Greek god Dionysus to a drinking party. Dionysus was the god of wine and was worshipped with special enthusiasm in vine-growing regions such as Athens, Boeotia and Naxos.

SERVICE
A carved relief shows servants carrying bowls of food. At formal banquets, the guests lay on their sides to eat as this was thought to aid digestion. The Greeks adopted this custom from the peoples of Asia. They often ate and drank until they passed out on their couches, leaving the servants to clear away without waking them.

4 Heat a teaspoon of the oil in the frying pan. Pour a quarter of the mix into the pan. Cook on both sides for about 4 minutes, until light brown.

5 Serve the pancake on a plate. Sprinkle on a handful of sesame seeds and pour extra honey over it. Cook the rest of the mix the same way.

Pancakes were a popular snack in ancient Greece, especially with theatre-goers. Food stalls were usually set up around theatres to catch the crowds who had come to view the latest play.

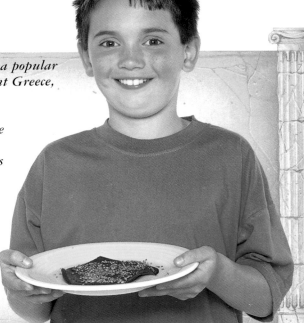

Women at Home

RESPECTABLE GREEK WOMEN were rarely seen out in the public domain. Their lives revolved around the household and family. From an early age, girls were trained in domestic skills which would enable them to run a household once married. A girl might be married off by her father at the age of 13 or 14. Her husband was usually much older and would be given a dowry to offset the costs of providing for her. The purpose of marriage was to produce a son to continue the husband's name. A wife assumed a number of responsibilities in her new home. If she was fortunate to have the help of slaves, she would direct them in their daily tasks. If not, she carried out those chores herself. Chores would include cooking meals, cleaning the house and caring for the children. Some women even managed the family finances.

"SO SHE SAID..."
Wealthy women were largely confined to their houses. They often relied on friends or household slaves for news about events in the outside world. Women from poorer families, without slaves, had to leave the house to shop and fetch water. Public fountains were popular meeting places for a gossip.

A CONSTANT TASK
Weaving was considered a respectable occupation for women. This vase painting shows Penelope, wife of the absent hero Odysseus, spinning wool into yarn. Women were expected to produce all the fabric needed to clothe their family. The material they spun was also used for household furnishings such as wall hangings.

KNUCKLEBONES
You will need: self-drying modelling clay, modelling tool, work board, cream paint, paintbrush.

1 Divide the self-drying modelling clay into 5 equal pieces. Roll each piece into a ball. Press each ball into a figure of eight shape, as above.

2 With the modelling tool, carve ridges around the middle of each shape. Make small dents in the end of each shape with your finger.

3 When the pieces have dried out, paint them. Use a cream coloured paint. Once the paint has dried, the pieces are ready to play with.

HOPING FOR HEALTH

Married women from wealthy families rarely left the house. When they did, it was usually to take part in family celebrations or religious ceremonies. The family shown on this carved relief from the 5th century BC are sacrificing a bull to Asclepius, god of health, and Hygieia, his daughter.

Knucklebones were made from the ankle-joints of small animals. These small bones were used in different ways, depending on the type of game. The Greeks also used the knucklebones as dice.

YOUR TURN

Women were supposed to be fully occupied with household tasks. But many kept slaves, which allowed them some leisure time. These women are playing knucklebones. Another favourite pastime was draughts, played on a board with 36 squares.

4 To play the game, gather together the five pieces into the palm of one hand. Throw them into the air. Quickly flip your hand over.

5 Try to catch the pieces on the back of your hand. If you're lucky and you catch them all, you win the game. If not, then the game continues.

6 Try to pick up the fallen pieces with the others still on the back of your hand. Throw them with your free hand and try to catch them again.

7 The winner is the first person to have all of the knucklebones on the back of their hand. It may take a few tries for you to get the hang of it.

Growing Up

CHILDREN FACED MANY OBSTACLES while growing up. When a baby was born, its father would decide whether to keep or abandon it. A sick or handicapped baby might be left outdoors at birth. Whoever rescued the child could raise it as their slave. Girls were more likely to be rejected because they could not provide for their parents in adulthood. Many children died in infancy through lack of health-care.

Education was considered to be important for boys. Even so, it was usually only sons of rich families who received a complete schooling. They were taught a variety of subjects, including reading, music and gymnastics. Boys from poorer families often learnt their father's trade. Education in domestic skills was essential for most girls. A notable exception was in Sparta, where girls joined boys in hard physical training.

BRINGING UP BABY
This baby is waving a rattle while sitting in a high chair. The chair also served as a potty. It might have wheels on it to help the baby learn how to walk.

BULLY OFF
These two boys are playing a game similar to hockey. On the whole, team sports were ignored in favour of sporting activities where an individual could excel. Wrestling and athletics are two such examples. They were encouraged as training for war.

YOU ARE IT
Two girls play a kind of tag game in which the loser has to carry the winner. Girls had less free time than boys did. They were supposed to stay close to home and help their mothers with housework, cooking and looking after the younger children.

MAKE A SCROLL
You will need: 2 x 30cm rods of balsa wood, 5cm in diameter, 4 doorknobs, double-sided sticky tape, sheet of paper 30cm x 30cm, 1 x 7cm rod of balsa wood, 2cm in diameter, craft knife, paintbrush, PVA glue, ink powder.

1 Carefully screw a door knob into either end of each 30cm rod of balsa wood, or ask an adult to do it for you. These are the end pieces of the scroll.

2 Cut two pieces of double-sided sticky tape 30cm long. Stick one piece of tape along the top of the paper and another along the bottom.

3 Wrap the top of the paper once around one of the pieces of balsa wood. Repeat this step again for the second piece at the bottom of the paper.

ACTION DOLL

The arms and legs on this terracotta figure are attached with cord so that the shoulders and knees can be moved. A doll such as this was a luxury item, which only a wealthy family could afford to buy for its children. Other popular toys were rattles and hoops.

THE ALPHABET

The first two of the Greek alphabet's 24 letters are called alpha and beta – these names give us the English word "alphabet".

Α Β Γ Δ Ε Ζ Η Θ Ι
A B G D E Z e TH I
Κ Λ Μ Ν Ξ Ο Π Ρ Σ
K L M N X O P R S
Τ Υ Φ Χ Ψ Ω
T U PH KH PS o

LIGHT OF LEARNING

This lamp takes the form of a teacher holding a scroll. Education involved learning poems and famous speeches from scrolls by heart. This was thought to help boys make effective speeches in court or public meetings. Good orators were always well thought of and could wield much influence.

Scrolls in ancient Greece were usually made from animal skin.

A SECOND MOTHER

Greeks often hired wet nurses (on the left) to breastfeed their babies. Some nurses were forbidden to drink wine in case it affected their milk or made them so drunk that they might harm the baby.

4 Ask an adult to help you with this step. Take the 7cm piece of balsa wood, and use your craft knife to sharpen the end of it into a point.

5 Paint the nib of your pen with glue. This will stop the wood from soaking up the ink. Add water to the ink powder to make ink.

6 Write some letters or a word on your scroll with your pen. We've translated the Greek alphabet above in the fact box. Use this as a guide.

7 We have copied out some letters in ancient Greek. You could also write a word. Ask a friend to translate what you have written, using the alphabet.

Greek Fashion

PHYSICAL BEAUTY AND AN ATTRACTIVE appearance were admired in ancient Greece in both men and women. Clothes were styled simply. Both sexes wore long tunics, draped loosely for comfort in the warm climate, and held in place with decorative pins or brooches. A heavy cloak was added for travelling or in bad weather. The tunics of soldiers and labourers were cut short, so they would not get in the way. Clothes were made of wool and linen, which were spun at home. Fabrics were coloured with dyes made from plants, insects and shellfish. The rich could afford more luxurious garments made from imported cotton or silk. Sandals were usually worn outdoors, though men sometimes wore boots. In hot weather hats made of straw or wool kept off the sun. A tan was not admired because it signified outdoor work as a labourer or a slave. Men wore their hair short, and women wore it long, coiled up in elaborate styles, sometimes decorated with ribbons.

SEE FOR YOURSELF

Glass mirrors were not known to the Greeks. Instead, they used highly polished bronze to see their reflection in. This mirror has a handle in the shape of a woman. Winged sphinxes sit on her shoulders.

GOLDEN LION

This heavy bracelet dates from around the 4th or 5th century BC. It is made of solid gold and decorated with two lion heads. Gold was valuable because there was little of to be found in Greece itself. st of it was imported from a Minor or Egypt.

KEEP IT SIMPLE

The figurine above is wearing a peplos. This was a simple, sleeveless dress worn by Greek women. The only adornment was a belt tied underneath the bust. This statue comes from a Greek colony in southern Italy.

CHITON

You will need: tape measure, rectangle of cloth, scissors, pins, chalk, needle, thread, 12 metal buttons (with loops), cord.

1 Ask a friend to measure your width from wrist to wrist, double this figure. Measure your length from shoulder to ankle. Cut your cloth to these figures.

2 Fold the fabric in half widthways. Pin the two sides together. Draw a chalk line along the fabric, 2cm away from the edge of the fabric.

3 Sew along the chalk line. Then turn the material inside out, so the seam is on the inside. Refold the fabric so the seam is at the back.

TEXTILE TRADE

Clothes in ancient Greece were usually made from wool and linen. The Greeks exported their wool, which was admired for its superior quality. Cotton and silk were imported to make clothes. But only wealthy Greeks could afford clothes made hese materials.

cotton

raw wool

linen

POWDER POT

Greek women used face powder and other cosmetics and kept them in a ceramic pot called a pyxis. This one was was made in Athens in about 450BC. The painted decoration shows women spinning and weaving.

Clothes were hand-made in ancient Greece. Enough material would be woven to fit the person they were being made for exactly, to avoid waste.

spiral band

BURIAL JEWELLERY

Some pieces of jewellery, like the ones pictured here, were made especially for burial. Very thin sheet gold wa beaten into belts and wreaths. Important people like the Kin and Queens of Macedonia were buried in crowns of gold leaves.

belt

wreath

4 Make a gap big enough for your head to fit in, at one of the open ends of the fabric. Mark where the gap is going to be and pin the fabric together there.

5 From the head gap mark a point every 5cm to the end of the fabric. Pin together the front and back along these points. Your arms will fit through here.

6 At each pin, sew on a button to hold the two sides of material together. To secure the button, sew through the loop several times and knot it.

7 Cut a length of cord, to fit around your waist with a little bit spare to tie. Tie this cord around your waist and bunch the material up, over the cord.

Gods and Goddesses

THE ANCIENT GREEKS BELIEVED that their gods looked like human beings and felt human emotions that led them to quarrel and fall in love. People also thought that the gods had magical powers and were immortal (meaning that they could live forever). With these powers, the gods could become invisible or disguise themselves and even turn people into animals. The gods were thought to influence all parts of human life and were kept busy with requests for help, from curing illness to ensuring a victory in war. In order to keep on the right side of the gods, individuals made sacrifices, left offerings and said prayers to them. Communities financed the building of temples, such as the Parthenon, paid for priests to look after them and organized festivals all in honour of the gods.

WILD GODDESS
Artemis was the goddess of wild places and animals, hunting and the moon. She was a skilful archer, whose arrows caused death and plagues. The power to heal was another of her attributes.

WINGED MESSENGER
Hermes was the god of eloquence and good luck. He was known for his mischievous and adventure-seeking nature. Zeus made him a messenger to the gods, to try and keep him occupied and out of trouble.

KING OF THE GODS
Zeus ruled over earth and heaven from Mount Olympus, (a real place on the border of Macedonia). He was thought to be a fair god who upheld order and justice. Wrongdoers could be punished with thunderbolts thrown by him.

PARTHENON
You will need: two pieces of white card 62cm by 38.5cm, ruler, black felt-tip pen, shoebox, scissors, blue, red and cream paint, paintbrush, PVA glue, piece of red corrugated card (approximately 39cm x 28.5cm), masking tape, craft knife, 160cm of balsa wood.

1 Draw a horizontal line across the centre of the card. Place the shoebox in the middle. Draw around it. Draw a second box 7cm away from this.

2 Draw a third box 2cm away from the second. Extend the lines of the second box to meet the third, to form four tabs, one in each corner.

3 To make the ends of the roof, draw half a diamond shape along the edge of the second box. Add on two rectangular tabs 1cm deep.

SYMBOLS

Each god and goddess was thought to be responsible for particular aspects of daily life. Each was represented by a symbol. Wheat symbolized Demeter, goddess of living things. Dionysus, god of the vine and wine, was appropriately represented by grapes.

wheat   *grapes*

LOVE AND PROTECTION

Aphrodite was the goddess of love and beauty. Her vanity was instrumental in causing one of the biggest campaigns in Greek folklore, the Trojan War. Aphrodite promised to win Paris (son of the king of Troy) the love of the most beautiful mortal woman in the world – Helen. In return, Paris was to name Aphrodite as the most beautiful of all the goddesses. However, Helen was already married to the king of Sparta. When she left him to join Paris, the Greeks declared war on Troy. A bloodthirsty war followed in which heroes and gods clashed.

GRAPES OF JOY

The god Dionysus was admired for his sense of fun. As god of fertility, the vine and wine, he was popular with both male and female worshippers. However, his followers were too enthusiastic for some city-states which banned celebrations in his name.

A POWERFUL FAMILY

Hera was the wife of Zeus and goddess of marriage. She was revered by women as the protector of their married lives. Her own marriage was marked by conflicts between herself and her husband. Her jealousy of rivals for her unfaithful husband's affections led her to persecute them. She was also jealous of Heracles, who was Zeus' son by another woman. Hera sent snakes to kill Heracles when he was a baby. Fortunately for Heracles, he had inherited his father's strength and killed the snakes before they harmed him.

4 Repeat step 3 for the other end of the roof. Cut out both ends of the roof and cut into the four corner tabs. Get your painting equipment ready.

5 Turn the roof piece over. Draw and then paint the above design on to each end piece. Paint a blue, 1cm margin along each side. Leave to dry.

6 Turn the card over. Fold up all the sides of the second box. Fold in each corner tab and glue to its adjoining side. Fold down the rectangular tabs.

7 Cut the piece of red corrugated card in half. Stick them together with tape, along the unridged side. Turn them over and fold along the middle.

Temples and Festivals

FESTIVALS TO HONOUR THE GODS were important public occasions in ancient Greece. At the heart of each festival was a temple. At festival time, people flocked to the cities from the countryside. The greatest festivals were occasions of splendour and celebration. They involved processions, music, sports, prayers, animal sacrifices and offerings of food, all of which took place at the temple. The earliest Greek temples were built of wood, and none have survived. Later, temples built from stone echoed the simplicity of tree trunks in their columns and beams. The finest temples were made from marble. They were often decorated with brightly painted friezes, showing mythical stories of gods, goddesses and heroes. No expense was spared because temples were thought to be the gods' earthly homes. Each temple housed a statue of the god to which it was dedicated. The statues were usually elaborate and occasionally made from precious materials such as gold and ivory.

A WOMAN'S ROLE
This vase in the shape of a woman's head was made about 600BC, probably for a temple dedicated to Apollo. Religion was one of the few areas of life outside the home in which women were allowed to take an active part. They served as priestesses in some cults and were often thought to have the gift of seeing into the future.

GRAND ENTRANCE
The monumental gateways to the temple complex on top of the Acropolis were called the Propylaea. The temple beside it honoured Athena who is shown as Nike, goddess of victory.

8 Glue the ends of the corrugated card to the folded up edges of the painted card. Leave to dry. This piece forms the roof to your temple.

9 Draw around the shoebox, on to the second piece of card. Draw another box 7cm away. Cut it out, leaving a 1cm border. This is the temple base.

10 Ask an adult to help you with this step. Cut out 32 columns from balsa wood. Each must be 5cm in height. Paint them cream and leave to dry.

11 Mark eight points along each edge of the second box by drawing around a column piece. Draw them an equal distance from each other.

A BIRTHDAY PARADE

A parade of horsemen, chariots and people leading sacrificial animals all formed part of the procession of the annual Panathenaic festival. It was held once a year, in Athens, to celebrate the goddess Athena's birthday. Every fourth year, the occasion involved an even more elaborate ceremony which lasted for six days. During the festivities, the statue of Athena was presented with a new robe.

A TEMPLE FOR THREE GODS

The Erectheum was built on the Acropolis, looking down on Athens 100 m below. Unusually for a Greek temple, it housed the worship of more than one god: the legendary king Erectheus; Athena, guardian goddess of the city of Athens, and Poseidon, god of the sea. The columns in the shape of women are called caryatids.

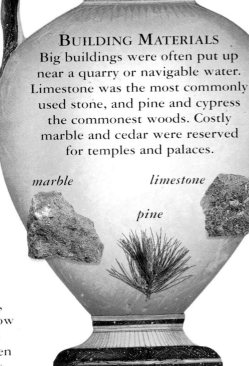

BUILDING MATERIALS

Big buildings were often put up near a quarry or navigable water. Limestone was the most commonly used stone, and pine and cypress the commonest woods. Costly marble and cedar were reserved for temples and palaces.

marble   *limestone*

pine

THE LION'S MOUTH

This gaping lion is actually a waterspout from an Athenian temple built in about 570BC. Although rainfall in Greece is low, waterspouts were necessary to allow storm water to drain off buildings with flat roofs. The lion was chosen as a symbol of strength and power.

12 Draw a door on to a short end of the shoebox. Glue the roof on to the top of the shoebox. Paint the 1cm border on the temple base, blue.

13 Glue the columns into place, between the roof and the base. Dab glue on to their ends. Position them on the circles marked out in step 11.

The magnificent Parthenon temple housed a 15m-high statue of Athena that was made of gold and ivory.

Heroes and Myths

GREEK MYTHOLOGY IS RICH in stories of victorious heroes and heroines, quarrelling gods and goddesses and mysterious and unusual creatures. While keeping people entertained, the stories also tried to answer questions about how the world and humans came into existence. These powerful tales provided inspiration for ancient Greek art and material for their plays. In addition to this, they served as a valuable historical record and encouraged the Greeks to take pride in their vibrant cultural past. Traditionally, mythical stories were passed down through generations by word of mouth. Sometimes travelling bards were paid to recite poems which they had learnt by heart. Eventually, these tales came to be written down. The earliest of these that survive are thought to be the work of the poet Homer. Two poems that we know about are *The Odyssey* and *The Iliad*. Both tell tales of heroes battling against supernatural forces.

MONSTER KILLER
According to Greek legend the Minotaur was half-bull and half-man. It lived in a maze called the labyrinth on the island of Crete. Many people had entered the maze but never come out. Each year the people of Athens were forced to send human sacrifices to feed the bull. The hero Theseus made it his mission to kill the Minotaur. A princess presented Theseus with a sword and a ball of string to help him. Theseus unwound the string as he walked through the maze. After killing the Minotaur he followed the string back to the entrance of the cave.

SNAKE STRANGLER
The super-strong Heracles was the only human being to become a Greek god. This Roman fresco shows him as a baby strangling serpents sent by the jealous goddess Hera to kill him.

HEAD OF MEDUSA
You will need: board, self-drying modelling clay, rolling pin, ruler, modelling tool, pencil, sandpaper, acrylic paints, one small and one large paintbrush, varnish (1 part water to 1 part PVA glue).

1 With a rolling pin, roll out a slab of clay 20cm by 20cm and 2cm thick. With the modelling tool, cut out a head in the shape shown in the picture.

2 Shape a small piece of clay into a nose. Mould it on to the head with your fingers. Use the modelling tool to smooth the edges into the face.

3 Carve a mouth with lots of teeth and two eyes and etch a gruesome design into the head. Press the end of a pencil into the eyes to make eyeballs.

STONY STARE

Medusa was a winged monster with hair of snakes. She was one of three such female gorgons. Medusa had a face so horrific that any human who looked directly at it was turned to stone. The only way to kill her was to cut off her head. Medusa, whose name means "cunning", outwitted several would-be killers. The hero Perseus finally killed her with help from Athena and Hermes. They lent Perseus a magic cap to make him invisible, a sickle to cut off Medusa's head and a shield in which to see her reflection. Even dead, Medusa remained powerful. Perseus killed his enemy Polydectes by forcing him to look at her face.

FOOLING THE GIANT

King Odysseus was a mythical hero who had many adventures. One escapade found him captured in a cave by a one-eyed giant. To escape, Odysseus stabbed out the giant's eye and rode out of the cave clinging to the underside of a ram.

The word gorgon in Greek suggests the monster's glaring eyes.

FLYING HORSE

The winged horse Pegasus appeared on the coins of Corinth as the city's symbol. Pegasus helped Bellerophon, a Corinthian hero, in his battles. First against the Chimaera which was a monster with a lion's head, a goat's middle and a snake's tail and then against the Amazons, a race of female warriors.

4 Between the palms of your hands, roll out four thin strips of clay to represent the snakes on Medusa's head. Press them into place as shown above.

5 Press a finger down on the end of each roll to make a snake's head. Use the modelling tool and pencil to carve in scales on the snakes' bodies.

6 The head needs to dry completely before you can paint the face. To dry it, let it sit for a few hours on either side. Be careful when you turn it over.

7 When the head is completely dry, sand with fine sandpaper. Paint the face in black, red, white and gold as shown here. Leave to dry and varnish.

Death and the Underworld

PEOPLE IN ANCIENT GREECE would live only about half as long as people in the West do today. It was common for sickly children to die in infancy. Large numbers of men were killed in battle, women often died in childbirth and epidemics could wipe out whole communities.

Most Greeks believed that after death, their souls roamed the Underworld, a cold and gloomy region where the wicked were sent to be punished. In *The Odyssey* the hero Achilles says, "I'd rather be a common labourer on Earth working for a poor man than lord of all the legions of the dead." Very few people, it was thought were good enough to be sent to the Isles of the Blessed. If they were, they could spend eternity amusing themselves with sports and music. People who had led exceptional lives (such as the hero Heracles) were thought destined to become gods and live on Mount Olympus.

When someone died, their body was either buried or cremated. The Greeks believed that only when the body or ashes had been covered with earth, could its spirit leave for the Underworld. Graves contained possessions for use in the afterlife, and women left offerings of food and drink at the graveside to help the spirits.

FRAGRANT FAREWELL
Graves were sometimes marked with lekythoi, white clay flasks holding a perfumed oil that had been used to anoint the body. The lekythoi were usually painted with farewell scenes, funerals or images of the dead.

A DIVE INTO THE UNKNOWN
The figure on the painting above is shown leaping from life into the ocean of death. The pillars were put up by Heracles to mark the end of the known, living world. This diver was found painted on the walls of a tomb.

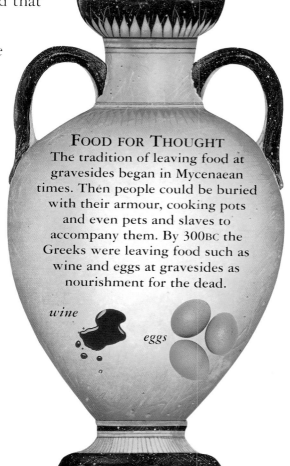

FOOD FOR THOUGHT
The tradition of leaving food at gravesides began in Mycenaean times. Then people could be buried with their armour, cooking pots and even pets and slaves to accompany them. By 300BC the Greeks were leaving food such as wine and eggs at gravesides as nourishment for the dead.

wine

eggs

TUG OF LOVE

This painting from a vase shows Persephone with Hades, her husband and ruler of the underworld. Hades dragged Persephone from earth down to the Underworld. Her distraught mother, the goddess Demeter, neglected the crops to search for her. Zeus intervened and decided that Persephone would spend six months of every year with her mother and the other six with Hades. Whenever her daughter returned in spring, Demeter would look after the crops. However, Demeter grew sad each time her daughter went back to the Underworld and wintertime would set in.

LAST JOURNEY

The body of a dead person was taken from their home to the grave by mourners bearing tributes. To express their grief, they might cut off their hair, tear at their cheeks with their nails until blood flowed, and wear black robes. If there was a funeral feast at the graveside, the dishes were smashed afterwards and left there.

ROYAL TOMB

Women were less likely to be honoured by tombstone portraits than men. Philis, seen above, was an exception to this rule, possibly because she was the daughter of a powerful Spartan king. Athens enforced a law against extravagant tombs. No more than 10 men could be employed for any more than three days to build one.

A Trip to the Theatre

THE FIRST GREEK DRAMAS were performed at temples in honour of the gods. The stories they told were a mixture of history and myth, and featured the adventures of famous Greeks as well as the exploits of gods and legendary heroes. The all-male cast was backed up by a chorus of singers and dancers, who provided a commentary on the action. Drama became so popular that large open-air theatres were built in major cities and at sacred places such as Delphi and Epidauros. Prizes were awarded to the best dramatists. The three most famous writers of tragedies were Aeschylus, Sophocles and Euripides. They wrote over 300 plays between them, but only a tenth survive. The works of another 150 known writers have all been lost. Greek drama is still performed in theatres today.

SEAT OF HONOUR
Most theatre-goers sat on stone benches. This carved chair might have been reserved for an important official or a sponsor who had paid the expenses of a public performance.

THEATRE
Large theatres like this one at Ephesus on the coast of modern Turkey had excellent acoustics and could hold an audience of over 10,000. The stage, a circle of beaten earth in the centre of the theatre, was called the orchestra, which means dancing floor.

BIRD MASK
You will need: balloon, petroleum jelly, papier-mâché (newspaper soaked in 1 part water to 2 parts PVA glue), black pen, scissors, paint, paintbrush, 2 pieces of ochre card (20cm x 10cm), glue stick, pair of compasses, two pieces of red card (40cm x 40cm), cord.

1 Blow up a balloon to head-size. Cover front and sides in petroleum jelly. Add several layers of papier-mâché. When this is dry, pop the balloon.

2 Ask a friend to mark the position of your eyes and the top of your ears on the mask. Cut out small holes at these points. Paint the mask as shown at the end.

3 Draw and cut out two beak shapes. Repeat for both pieces of ochre card. Mark a point 1cm along the bottom of the beak (the edge marked *a* above).

COMIC TURN

A figurine from the 2nd century BC shows a masked comic actor sitting on an altar. He is hiding in a temple to escape punishment. Comedies were much enjoyed, but considered inferior to tragedies.

PLAYING PARTS

Greek actors wore masks to represent different characters and emotions. The same actor could play different roles in one drama by changing his mask. All the players were male, but some took female roles. Women were not allowed on the stage, and may even have been barred from joining the audience.

SUFFERING COMEDY

In this comic scene the actor in the middle plays the part of a centaur called Cheiron. Centaurs were mythical creatures that were half-man and half-horse. Cheiron was the wisest of them all. But he was also seen as a figure of fun because he was immortal yet suffered from a fatal wound.

To wear your mask, thread a piece of cord through the holes on each side of the head. Tie them together at the back. This mask is modelled on an original worn by the chorus in Aristophanes' comedy, The Birds.

4 Draw a line from the corner of the top edge (*b*) to this point. Fold back the line. Glue the two pieces together along the top edge. Repeat.

5 Put the compass point in the corner of the red card. Draw two arcs, one with a 10cm radius and one with a 20cm radius. Cut out as one piece.

6 Cut feather shapes into the top of the red card. Draw an arc 5cm from the bottom. Cut out 14 tabs, as shown. Repeat both steps for the other piece of card.

7 Glue the two red cards together at the top. Glue the tabs down on to the top of the mask. Glue the beak pieces to the mask. Draw on the eyes.

Music and Dance

MUSIC AND DANCE WERE BOTH AN important part of Greek life. People sang, played and danced at religious ceremonies. Music was enjoyed for pleasure and entertainment at family celebrations, dramatic performances, feasts and drinking parties. Few written records remain of the notes played, but examples of the instruments do. The most popular instruments were the pipes. They were wind instruments similar to the oboe or clarinet. One pipe on its own was called the *aulos*, two played together were known as *auloi*. The stringed lyre and flute were other popular instruments. The stringed lyre produced solemn and dignified music. It was often played by men of noble birth to accompany a poetry recital. The flute was more usually played by slaves or dancing girls.

BREATH CONTROL
The leather strap tied around the auloi-player's cheeks helped to focus the power of his breath. One tube of the auloi supplied the melody, while the other produced an accompanying drone to give more depth to the sound. The aulos had as few as three or as many as 24 fingerholes for making the different notes.

Greek soldiers complained that lack of music was a hardship of war. Spartan soldiers resolved this problem by blowing tunes on pipes as they marched. Music was believed to have magical powers. Greek legend tells of Orpheus soothing savage beasts by playing his lyre. Another myth tells how Amphion (a son of Zeus) made stones move on their own and built a wall around the city of Thebes, by playing his lyre.

BANG! CRASH!
The bronze figurine above is playing the cymbals. They made a sound similar to castanets. The Greeks used the cymbals to accompany dancing. Other percussion instruments included wooden clappers and hand-held drums, like tambourines.

TIMPANON
You will need: scissors, corrugated card, tape measure, plate, white card, pair of compasses, pencil, PVA glue, tape, strips of newspaper, cream paper, red and purple felt-tip pens, ochre card, red and yellow ribbons.

1 Cut out a strip of corrugated card 5cm wide. Wrap it around a dinner plate. Add 6cm on to the length of this card and cut it off.

2 Put the plate upside down on the white card. Draw around it. Draw another circle 3cm inside the first. Cut this out to make a ring.

3 Glue the cardboard strip that you made in step 1 to the edge of the cardboard ring you made in step 2. Then tape them together for extra hold.

50

DIVINE MUSIC

Terpsichore was one of the Nine Muses, or spirits of the arts. She was the spirit of dance and music. Here Terpsichore plays a harp while her attendants hold the lyre and auloi. Other Muses included Polyhymnia, the spirit of hymns, and Euterpe, the spirit of flute-playing.

PERCUSSION

The timpanon was a tambourine made of animal skin, stretched over a frame. It was tapped to provide rhythmic accompaniment at dances or recitals. Stringed and wind instruments were thought superior because they made fitting music for solemn or exclusive occasions. Drums, cymbals and clappers were associated with buskers.

ENTERTAINING

In this plate painting a young man plays the auloi while his female companion dances. Professional musicians were often hired to entertain guests at dinner parties. Sometimes the musicians were household slaves.

To play the timpanon tap on it with your fingers, as the ancient Greeks would have done.

4 Make up some papier mâché solution with 1 part glue to 2 parts water. Soak strips of newspaper in it and cover the card ring with the wet strips.

5 Draw around the plate on to cream paper. Draw another circle 5cm outside this. To make tabs, cut out about 28 small triangles around the edge.

6 Draw the design shown above on to the paper. Place the paper over the top of the card ring. Dab glue on each tab and stick on to the corrugated card.

7 Cut a strip of ochre card big enough to fit around the timpanon. Decorate it as above and glue on. Make 4 bows with the ribbons and glue around the edge.

Arts and Crafts

THE ARTISTS AND CRAFTWORKERS of ancient Greece were admired for the quality of their work. They produced many objects of art including beautiful pottery, fine jewellery and impressive sculptures. Materials they worked with included stone, gold, silver, glass, gemstones and bronze. They also used wood, leather, bone, ivory and horn. Most goods were made on a small scale in workshops surrounding the market-place (*agora*). A craftsman might work on his own or with the help of his family and a slave or two. In the larger workshops of such cities as Athens, slaves laboured to produce bulk orders of popular goods. These might include shields, pottery and metalwork which were traded around the Mediterranean Sea for a large profit.

BULK PRODUCTION
Above is a terracotta mould, and on the right, the casting taken from it. Making a mould was a skilled and time-consuming task. Using a mould made it possible to produce items faster and more cheaply than carving each piece individually.

RAW MATERIALS
Gold was an expensive import and was usually used to make luxury items such as jewellery. Less commonly, it was used to decorate statues and to make gold coins. Clay was used in the production of a wide range of craft goods from vases to statuettes.

clay

gold

PANATHENAIC VASE
You will need: balloon, bowl, PVA glue, water, newspaper, two rolls of masking tape, black pen, scissors, sheet of paper 42cm x 30cm, card, pencil, paintbrush, black and cream paint.

1 Blow up the balloon. Cover it with two layers of papier mâché (paper soaked in one part glue, two parts water). Leave on one side to dry.

2 Using a roll of masking tape as a guide, draw and cut out two holes at the top and bottom of the balloon. Throw away the burst balloon.

3 Roll the sheet of paper into a tube. Make sure that it will fit through the middle of the roll of masking tape. Secure the tube with tape or glue.

VASE PAINTING

Black-figure vase painting originated in Corinth around 700BC. The black-figure style was succeeded by a red-figure style invented in Athens around 525BC. The painters were not all anonymous artisans. Many were widely recognized as artists in their own right who signed their works. The export of vases like this became a major source of income for both cities.

HOT WORK

In this scene two blacksmiths are forging metal at a brick furnace. Metal goods were expensive to produce. The furnaces themselves were fuelled by charcoal (burnt wood) which was expensive to make because wood was scarce in Greece. In addition, supplies of metal often had to be imported, sometimes from great distances. For example, tin, which was mixed with local copper to make bronze, was brought from southern Spain.

Amphorae like this one were given as prizes at the Panathenaic games. They were decorated with sporting images.

GOLD PECTORAL

This gold pectoral, made on the island of Rhodes in the 7th century BC, was meant to be worn across the breast. Gold was rare in Greece. It was usually imported at great expense from surrounding areas such as Egypt or Asia Minor.

4 Push the tube through the middle of the balloon. Tape into place. Push a roll of masking tape over the bottom of the paper tube and tape.

5 Tape the second roll of masking tape to the top of the tube. Make sure that both rolls are securely attached at either end of the paper tube.

6 Cut two strips of card, 15cm long. Attach them to either side of the vase, as seen above. Cover the entire vase with papier mâché, and leave to dry.

7 Using a pencil, copy the pattern seen on the vase in the picture above on to your vase. Carefully paint in the pattern and leave on one side to dry.

53

Sports and Fitness

FITNESS WAS VALUED as an essential preparation for war. But the Greeks also enjoyed sport for its own sake, and most cities had a public gymnasium, where men gathered to train and to relax. They preferred individual contests to team games, and often celebrated religious festivals by running races to honour the gods. This is how the Olympic Games first began in 776BC. It was held every four years, and expanded to include long jump, throwing the discus and javelin, boxing, wrestling, chariot races and horse races, as well as poetry and drama competitions. There was also a gruesome fighting sport called *pankration* (total power), a combination of boxing and wrestling in which the only forbidden tactics were eye-gouging and biting. During the Olympics, all wars between cities stopped, so that people could journey safely to the Games. Women were banned from competing or watching the Olympics but they had their own games, also held at Olympia in honour of the goddess Hera.

THE WINNER

A Greek king (on the right) hands a wreath of victory to an Olympic winner. A priest stands by to remind contestants that they are on sacred ground. There were no cash prizes at the Olympics. However, because they brought honour to their cities, winners were sometimes given money on their return home, or even free meals for life.

SPORTING STARS

This vase painting shows a long-jumper holding weights, a discus thrower and two men with javelins. They represent three of the five sports that made up the *pentathlon* (*penta* is Greek for five). The other two were running and wrestling. The pentathlon began with a foot race, which was followed by javelin throwing, then discus throwing and finished with the long jump. The two contestants who scored highest in these events then wrestled one another to decide the overall winner. Most sportsmen were amateurs. There were also many professionals who trained and competed for a single event.

SPORTING FACILITIES

Much of ancient Olympia, where the first Olympic Games were held, has been uncovered by archaeologists working there since 1829. There were many facilities serving the competitors and spectators. At the centre of the complex were two large temples dedicated to Hera and Zeus. Amongst the buildings surrounding the temples were a hostel, restaurants, a huge gymnasium for training in and a hippodrome for horse and chariot races. Despite its size, Olympia never became a city, because it had no permanent citizens or local government.

DANGEROUS GAME

At the end of a chariot race, an armed man jumped off of the moving vehicle and ran a foot race. This event was eventually dropped from the Games because it often provoked laughter at undignified accidents instead of admiration for the competitors' skill. Chariots frequently overturned with disastrous results. As many as 40 competitors might take part, racing 12 laps of a 1,100 m circuit. The winner was the owner of the chariot and horses, not the driver.

GOING THE DISTANCE

Long-jumpers carried heavy weights to give them more momentum. The weights also helped them to balance. They jumped on to a bed of crumbled earth (skamma) raked smooth. This helped them to avoid injuries and leave a clear footprint so that the judges could measure the distance they had covered.

STEP THIS WAY

Competitors taking part in the original Olympic Games entered the stadium through this archway. The grassy embankments surrounding the stadium could seat up to 40,000 spectators.

GETTING READY

An athlete binds his hair with a cloth to keep it out of the way. Most athletes competed naked in the Olympic Games. It was felt that sport glorified male strength and beauty. When women competed against each other in the games to honour Hera, they wore short tunics.

Science and Philosophy

THE GREEKS COULD AFFORD to devote time to studying and thinking because their civilization was both wealthy and secure. They learned astrology from the Babylonians, and mathematics from the Egyptians. They used their scientific knowledge to develop many practical inventions, including water clocks, cogwheels, gearing systems, slot machines and steam engines. However, these devices were not widely used as there were many slave workers to do the jobs.

The word "philosophy" comes from the Greek word *philosophos*, meaning love of knowledge. The Greeks developed many different branches of philosophy. Three of these were politics (how best to govern), ethics (how to behave well) and cosmology (how the universe worked).

Greek philosophers recognized the value of experimenting. But they could not always see their limitations. Aristotle discovered that evaporation turned salt water into fresh water, and wrongly assumed wine would turn into water by the same process.

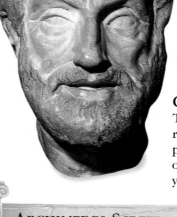

GREAT THINKER
The philosopher Aristotle (384–322BC) is often recognized as the founder of Western science. He pioneered a rational approach to the world, based on observing and recording evidence. For three years, he was the tutor of Alexander the Great.

CLOCK TOWER
The Tower of the Winds in Athens contains a water clock. The original Egyptian invention was a bucket of water with a tiny hole in the bottom. As the water dripped out of it, the water level fell past scored marks on the inside of the bucket, measuring time. The Greeks improved on this design, using the flow of water to work a dial with a moving pointer.

ARCHIMEDES SCREW
You will need: clean, empty plastic bottle, scissors, modelling clay, strong tape, length of clear plastic tube, bowl of water, blue food colouring, empty bowl.

1 Cut off the bottle top. Place the modelling clay into the middle of the bottle, about 5cm from the end. Punch a hole here with the scissors.

2 Cut a strip of tape the same length as the bottle. Tape it to the middle of the bottle. This will give the tube extra grip later on.

3 Twist the length of tube around the bottle. Go from one end of the bottle to the other. Tape the tube into place over the first piece of tape.

WATER LIFTER

When the Archimedes screw is turned, it lifts water from one level to another. It is named after its inventor, the scientist Archimedes, who lived about 287–211BC, in Syracuse, Sicily. It is still in use today.

FATHER OF GEOMETRY

Euclid (about 330–260BC) was a mathematician. He lived in the Greek-Egyptian city of Alexandria. He is known as the father of geometry, which comes from the Greek word for "measuring land". Geometry is the study of points, lines, curves, surfaces and their measurements. His geometry textbook was called *Elements*. It was still widely used in the early part of the 20th century AD, over 2,000 years after his death. This picture shows the front page of an edition of the book that was printed in London in 1732.

4 Place a few drops of the blue food colouring into the bowl of water. Stir it in so that the colour mixes evenly throughout the water.

5 Place one end of the bottle into the bowl of blue water. Make sure that the tube at the opposite end is pointing towards the empty bowl.

6 Twist the bottle around in the blue water. As you do so, you will see the water start travelling up the tube and gradually filling the other bowl.

The invention of the Archimedes screw made it possible for farmers to water their fields with irrigation channels. It saved them from walking back and forth to the river with buckets.

Medical Matters

THE GREEKS BELIEVED THAT ultimately only the gods had the power to heal wounds and cure sickness. But they also developed a scientific approach to medicine. Greek doctors could treat injuries and battle wounds by bandaging and bone-setting. They relied on rest, diet and herbal drugs to cure disease. However, they were powerless against large-scale epidemics, such as the plague. Doctors believed that good health was dependent on the balance between four main body fluids – blood, phlegm and yellow and black bile. If this balance was disturbed, they attempted to restore it by applying heated metal cups to the body to draw off harmful fluids. The sweat this produced convinced them it worked. This mistaken practice continued in Europe until the 17th century.

FATHER OF MEDICINE
Hippocrates founded a medical school around 400BC. He taught that observation of symptoms was more important than theory. His students took an oath to use their skills to heal and never to harm.

BODY BALANCE
Bleeding was a common procedure, intended to restore the body's internal balance. This carving shows surgical instruments and cups used for catching blood. Sometimes bleeding may have helped to drain off poisons, but more often it can only have weakened the patient.

HEALING GOD
The Greeks worshipped Asclepius, as the god of healing. He is shown here with a serpent, representing wisdom. Invalids seeking a cure made a visit to his shrine.

LEG OFFERING
You will need: self-drying modelling clay, rolling pin, board, ruler, modelling tool, paintbrush, cream acrylic paint.

1 Divide the clay into two pieces. With the rolling pin, roll out one piece to 15cm length, 10cm width and 2cm depth. This is the base for the leg.

2 Roll out the second piece of clay. With the modelling tool, carve out a leg and foot shape. It should be big enough to fit on one side of the base.

3 Gently place the leg on the right-hand side of the base. With the tool, draw a shallow outline around the leg into the base. Remove the leg.

THEORY AND PRACTICE

Patients would explain their dreams to doctors, who then prescribed treatment. In this relief, a healing spirit in the shape of a serpent visits a sleeping patient. In the foreground, the physician bandages the wounded arm.

NATURAL HEALING

The Greeks used a large variety of natural treatments to cure illnesses. Herbal remedies were particularly popular. Lentils, mustard and honey may have been combined in a poultice and applied to a wound.

lentils

mustard

honey

TOOL KIT

The Greeks used bronze surgical instruments, including forceps and probes. Surgery was usually a last resort. Even when it was successful, patients often died from the shock and pain, or from infection afterwards. Operations on limbs were more successful than those on body cavities such as the chest or stomach.

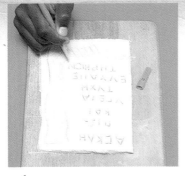

4 With the tool, score the outline with lines. Carve the ancient Greek message seen in the picture above next to the leg.

5 Mould the leg onto the scored area of the base. Use your fingers to press the sides of the leg in place. Carve toes and toenails into the foot.

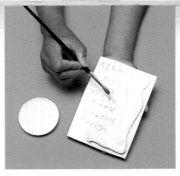

6 Paint over the entire leg offering with a cream colour, to give it an aged look. Leave to dry overnight. Your leg offering is done.

This model is based on a real one left as a thank-offering to the god Asclepius by someone whose leg was affected by illness. This was a common practice in ancient Greece.

Fighting Forces

ALL GREEK MEN were expected to fight in their city's army. In Sparta the army was on duty all year round. In other parts of Greece men gave up fighting in autumn to bring in the harvest and make the wine. The only full-time soldiers in these states were the personal bodyguards of a ruler or mercenaries who fought for anyone who paid them. Armies consisted mainly of hoplites (armoured infantry), cavalry (soldiers on horseback) and a group of foot soldiers armed with stones and bows and arrows. The hoplites were the most important fighting force as they engaged in hand-to-hand combat. The cavalry was less effective in war because riders had no stirrups, which made charging with a lance impossible, as the rider would fall off on contact. They were used for scouting, harassing a beaten enemy and carrying messages.

HARD HELMET
This bronze helmet from Corinth was fashioned to protect the face. It has guards for the cheeks and the bridge of the nose. Iron later replaced bronze as the main metal for weapons.

BOWMEN
The Greek army usually employed Scythian archers to fight for them. Archers were useful for fighting in mountainous countryside where they could position themselves above the enemy. Some Greeks soldiers did fight with bows and arrows. They fought in small units known as *psiloi*. But most of the soldiers in these units could only afford simple missile weapons, such as a javelin or slings from which they shot stones.

WARRIOR GREAVES
You will need: clear film, bowl of water, plaster bandages; sheet of paper, kitchen paper, scissors, cord, gold paint, paintbrush.

1 Ask a friend to help you with steps 1 to 3. Loosely cover both of your lower legs (from your ankle to the top of your knee) in clear film.

2 Soak each plaster bandage in water. Working from one side of your leg to the other, smooth the bandage over the front of each leg.

3 Carefully remove each greave. Set them on some paper. Dampen some kitchen paper and use it to smooth the greaves down. Leave them to dry.

A Rare Sight in Battle

Chariots were not often used in warfare because they could only be used on flat plains. There were usually two people in the chariot, one to drive it, and the other to fight from the back of it.

Fighting Forces

Tin and copper were used to make bronze, the main material for weapons and armour. Bronze is harder than pure copper and, unlike iron, does not rust. As there was no tin in Greece, it was imported from faraway lands.

copper   *tin*

Hoplites

This fighting force was made up of middle-class men who could afford the weaponry. A hoplite's armoury consisted of a shield, helmet, spear, sword and greaves. Helmets were made of bronze and were usually crested with horsehair. The body was protected by a bronze cuirass, a one-piece breast- and back-plate, under which the hoplites wore a leather cuirass. Shields were usually round and decorated with a symbol.

4 Trim the edges of the greaves, to make them look neat. Measure four lengths of cord to fit around your leg, below the knee and above the ankle.

5 Turn the greaves on to their front. Lay the cord in place at the point where you want to tie them to your leg. Fix them into place using wet bandages.

6 Leave the plaster bandages to dry, with the cord in place. Now paint each greave with gold paint. Once they are dry, tie them on.

Greaves were attached to the lower leg to protect it in battle. They were worn by hoplites.

Warfare

WHEN THE GREEKS WENT TO WAR it was usually to engage in raids and sieges of rival city-states. Major battles with foreign powers were rare, but the results could be devastating. Army commanders had to choose their ground with care and rely on the discipline and training of their troops to carry through their overall plan. Once the fighting had started, it was almost impossible to control large masses of men or to change their orders. The death or flight of a few key leaders could cause a whole army to break up in chaos.

The core of a Greek army consisted of heavily armed foot soldiers (hoplites) who fought together in solid blocks called phalanxes. As long as they stayed calm, the soldiers were protected by their bristling spears, overlapping shields and sheer weight of numbers. If they panicked and broke up, it was easy for the enemy to pick off individual hoplites, weighed down by 30 kg of armour.

HEROES AT PLAY
Achilles and Ajax were legendary Greek heroes of the Trojan war. This vase shows them playing dice. This game was played by soldiers to while away the time or to decide the share-out of loot. The outcome of the game was sometimes interpreted as a symbol of fate and death.

GREEK TRICK
The Greeks ended the siege of Troy by leaving a wooden horse outside the city and pretending to sail away. The Trojans dragged the horse inside, not realizing that it was filled with Greek soldiers. The soldiers crept out of the horse at night and opened the city gates to let their comrades in. Together they overran the city.

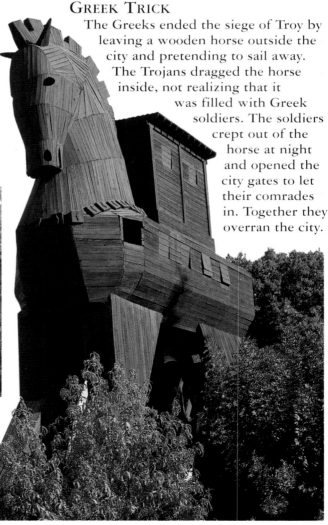

CLOSE COMBAT
The Greek soldiers and heroes of Homer's time fought each other in a series of one-to-one duels. In this engraving, Greek and Trojan warriors are fighting hand to hand. However, as armies began to use more hoplites, methods of fighting changed to accommodate them. This involved men fighting together in a phalanx.

VICTORY AGAINST THE ODDS

At the battle of Issus in 333BC Alexander the Great (left) led the charge against the Persian king Darius (in the chariot). Darius fled in panic, and his much larger army broke up. The Persian army was made up of many different peoples from all over his vast empire. They spoke different languages and did not trust each other, making control harder. In contrast, Alexander had tight control and long experience of fighting with his troops.

SEA FIGHT

In 480BC, the battle of Salamis ended a Persian invasion into Greek territory. The Persians had more and faster ships, but the Greeks defeated them by luring them into narrow waters where these advantages were lost. Then the crowded Persian vessels were rammed to pieces by the much heavier Greek ships.

END OF AN EMPIRE

Greece won another decisive victory against Persia in 331BC. At the battle of Gaugemala the Persian cavalry outnumbered Alexander's almost five to one and the infantry two to one. Discipline, daring and determination overcame the odds and the Persian army lost the battle. Consequently, the Persian empire finally yielded to Alexander.

THE ROMANS

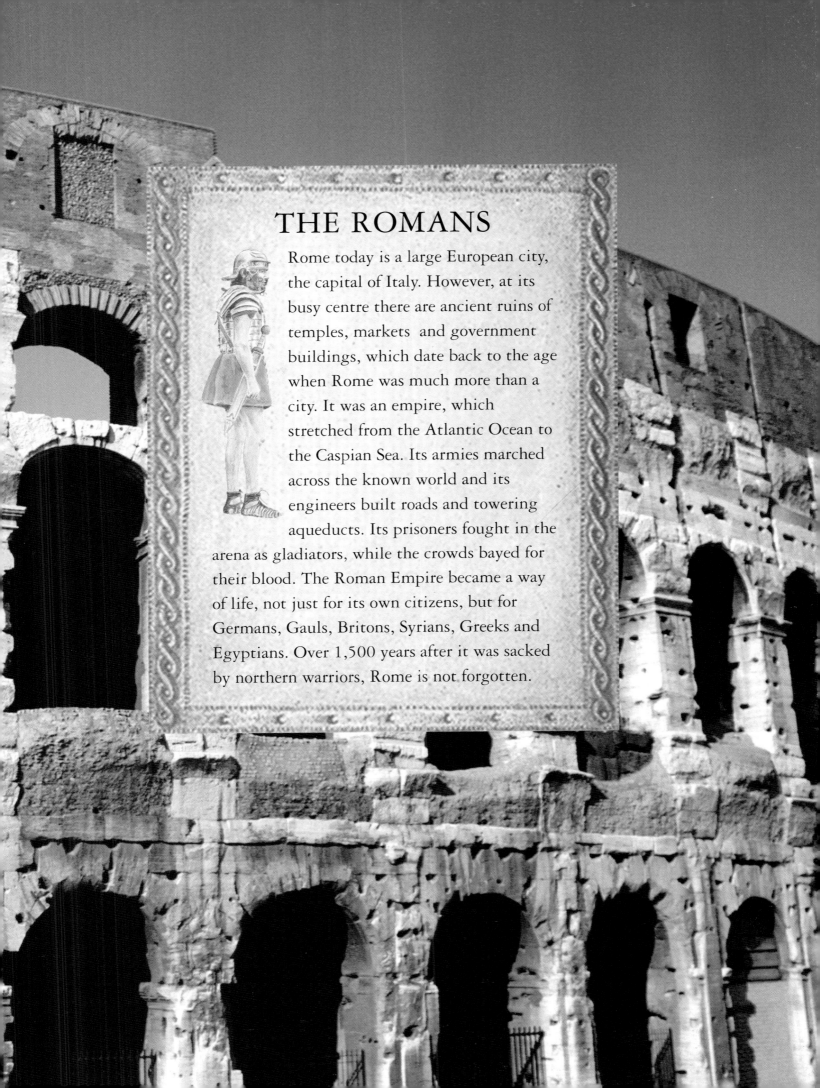

Rome today is a large European city, the capital of Italy. However, at its busy centre there are ancient ruins of temples, markets and government buildings, which date back to the age when Rome was much more than a city. It was an empire, which stretched from the Atlantic Ocean to the Caspian Sea. Its armies marched across the known world and its engineers built roads and towering aqueducts. Its prisoners fought in the arena as gladiators, while the crowds bayed for their blood. The Roman Empire became a way of life, not just for its own citizens, but for Germans, Gauls, Britons, Syrians, Greeks and Egyptians. Over 1,500 years after it was sacked by northern warriors, Rome is not forgotten.

The Story of Rome

THE CITY OF ROME today is a bustling place, full of traffic and crowds. But if you could travel back in time to around 800BC, you would find only a few small villages on peaceful, wooded hillsides along the banks of the river Tiber. According to legend, Rome was founded here in 753BC. In the centuries that followed, the Romans came to dominate Italy and the Mediterranean. They farmed and traded and fought for new lands. Rome grew to become the centre of a vast empire that stretched across Europe into Africa and Asia. The Empire lasted for centuries and brought a sophisticated way of life to vast numbers of people. Many Roman buildings and artefacts still survive to show us what life was like in the Roman Empire.

ROMAN ITALY
As the city of Rome prospered, the Romans gradually conquered neighbouring tribes. By 250BC they controlled most of Italy. This map shows some of the important towns and cities of that time.

ANCIENT AND MODERN
In Rome today, people live alongside the temples, marketplaces and public buildings of the past. This is the Colosseum, a huge arena called an amphitheatre. It was used for staging games and fights, and first opened to the public in AD80.

TIMELINE 753BC–276BC

Rome's rise to power was sudden and spectacular. Its eventful history includes bloody battles, eccentric emperors, amazing inventions and remarkable feats of engineering. The Roman Empire prospered for almost 500 years, and still influences the way we live today.

Romulus, the first king of Rome

c.753BC The city of Rome is founded by Romulus, according to legend.

673–641BC Tullus Hostilius, Rome's third king, expands the city's territory by conquering a neighbouring settlement. Rome's population doubles as a result.

641–616BC Pons Sublicius, the first bridge across the river Tiber, is constructed.

The harbour town of Ostia is founded at the mouth of the Tiber.

600BC The Latin language is first written in a script that is still used today.

inscription in Latin, carved in stone

750BC   700BC   650BC   600BC

CLUES TO THE PAST
The coin on this necklace dates from the reign of the Emperor Domitian, AD81–96. Gold does not rot like wood and other materials, so jewellery like this can give us clues about Roman craft methods, changing fashions, trade and even warfare.

ARCHAEOLOGISTS AT WORK
These archaeologists are excavating sections of wall plaster from the site of a Roman house in Britain. Many remains of Roman buildings and artefacts, as well as books and documents, have survived from that time. These all help us build up a picture of what life was like in the Roman Empire.

SECRETS BENEATH THE SEA
Divers have discovered Roman shipwrecks deep under the waters of the Mediterranean Sea. Many have their cargo still intact. These jars were being transported over 2,000 years ago. By examining shipwrecks, archaeologists can learn how Roman boats were built, what they carried and where they traded.

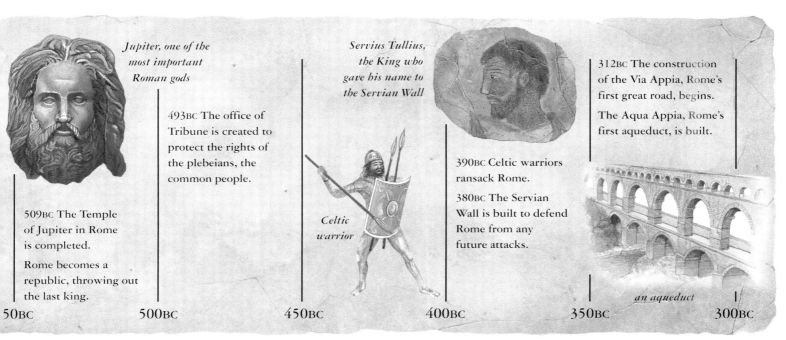

Jupiter, one of the most important Roman gods

Servius Tullius, the King who gave his name to the Servian Wall

312BC The construction of the Via Appia, Rome's first great road, begins.

The Aqua Appia, Rome's first aqueduct, is built.

493BC The office of Tribune is created to protect the rights of the plebeians, the common people.

390BC Celtic warriors ransack Rome.

380BC The Servian Wall is built to defend Rome from any future attacks.

509BC The Temple of Jupiter in Rome is completed.

Rome becomes a republic, throwing out the last king.

Celtic warrior

an aqueduct

550BC   500BC   450BC   400BC   350BC   300BC

The Great Empire

B Y THE YEAR AD117, the Roman Empire was at its height. It was possible to travel 4,000km from east to west and still hear the trumpets of the Roman legions. As a Roman soldier you might have had to shiver in the snowy winters of northern Britain, or sweat and toil in the heat of the Egyptian desert.

The peoples of the Empire were very different. There were Greeks, Egyptians, Syrians, Jews, Africans, Germans and Celts. Many of them belonged to civilizations that were already ancient when Rome was still a group of villages. Many revolted against Roman rule, but uprisings were quickly put down. Gradually, conquered peoples came to accept being part of the Empire. From AD212 onwards, any free person living under Roman rule had the right to claim "I am a Roman citizen". Slaves, however, had very few rights.

In AD284, after a series of violent civil wars, this vast empire was divided into several parts. Despite being reunited by the Emperor Constantine in AD324, the Empire was doomed. A hundred years later, the western part was invaded by fierce warriors from the north, with disastrous consequences. Although the Western Empire came to an end in AD476, the eastern part continued until 1453. The Latin language survived, used by the Roman Catholic Church and by scientists and scholars in Europe. It is still learned today, and is the basis of languages such as Italian, Spanish, French and Romanian.

BRITAIN

London

FRANCE

SPAIN

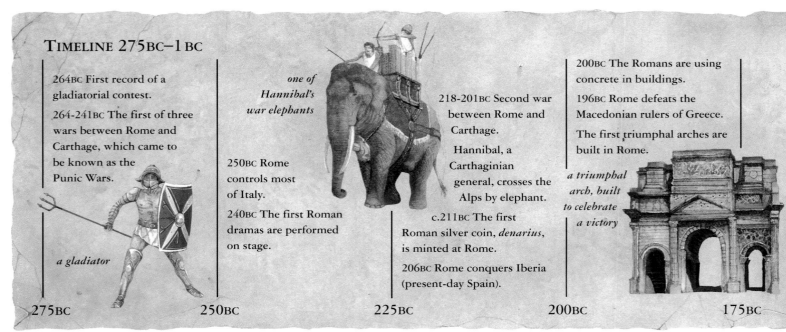

TIMELINE 275BC–1 BC

264BC First record of a gladiatorial contest.

264-241BC The first of three wars between Rome and Carthage, which came to be known as the Punic Wars.

a gladiator

one of Hannibal's war elephants

250BC Rome controls most of Italy.

240BC The first Roman dramas are performed on stage.

218-201BC Second war between Rome and Carthage.

Hannibal, a Carthaginian general, crosses the Alps by elephant.

c.211BC The first Roman silver coin, *denarius*, is minted at Rome.

206BC Rome conquers Iberia (present-day Spain).

200BC The Romans are using concrete in buildings.

196BC Rome defeats the Macedonian rulers of Greece.

The first triumphal arches are built in Rome.

a triumphal arch, built to celebrate a victory

275BC 250BC 225BC 200BC 175BC

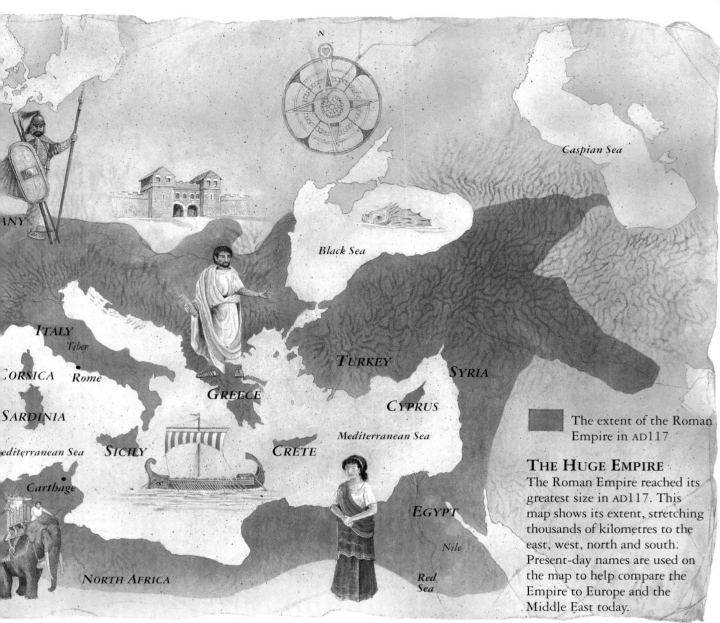

N

Caspian Sea

Black Sea

ANY

ITALY
Tiber

CORSICA • Rome

SARDINIA

Mediterranean Sea

SICILY

Carthage

NORTH AFRICA

GREECE

TURKEY

SYRIA

CYPRUS

Mediterranean Sea

CRETE

EGYPT

Nile

Red Sea

The extent of the Roman Empire in AD117

THE HUGE EMPIRE

The Roman Empire reached its greatest size in AD117. This map shows its extent, stretching thousands of kilometres to the east, west, north and south. Present-day names are used on the map to help compare the Empire to Europe and the Middle East today.

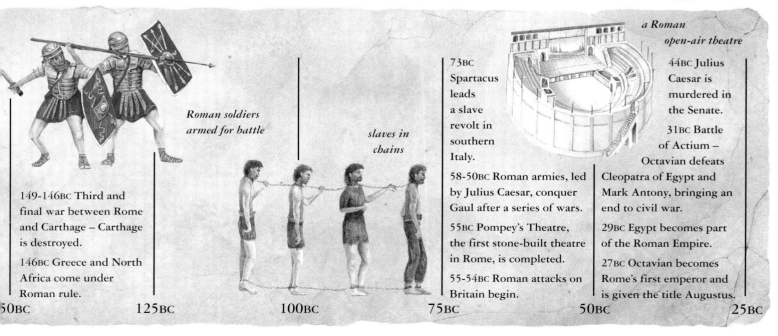

Roman soldiers armed for battle

slaves in chains

73BC Spartacus leads a slave revolt in southern Italy.

58-50BC Roman armies, led by Julius Caesar, conquer Gaul after a series of wars.

55BC Pompey's Theatre, the first stone-built theatre in Rome, is completed.

55-54BC Roman attacks on Britain begin.

a Roman open-air theatre

44BC Julius Caesar is murdered in the Senate.

31BC Battle of Actium – Octavian defeats Cleopatra of Egypt and Mark Antony, bringing an end to civil war.

29BC Egypt becomes part of the Roman Empire.

27BC Octavian becomes Rome's first emperor and is given the title Augustus.

149-146BC Third and final war between Rome and Carthage – Carthage is destroyed.

146BC Greece and North Africa come under Roman rule.

50BC   125BC   100BC   75BC   50BC   25BC

The Roman World

THE PEOPLE who made Roman history came from many different backgrounds. The names of the famous survive on monuments and in books. There were consuls and emperors, successful generals and powerful politicians, great writers and historians. However, it was thousands of ordinary people who really kept the Roman Empire going – merchants, soldiers of the legions, tax collectors, servants, farmers, potters, and others like them.

Many of the most famous names of that time were not Romans at all. There was the Carthaginian general, Hannibal, Rome's deadliest enemy. There were also Celtic chieftains and queens, such as Vercingetorix, Caractacus and Boudicca.

ROMULUS AND REMUS
According to legend, Romulus was the founder and first king of Rome. The legend tells how he and his twin brother Remus were abandoned as babies. They were saved by a she-wolf, who looked after them until they were found by a shepherd.

AUGUSTUS (63BC–AD14)
Augustus, born Octavian, was the great-nephew and adopted son of Julius Caesar. After Caesar's death, he took control of the army. He became ruler of the Roman world after defeating Mark Antony at the Battle of Actium in 31BC. In 27BC, he became Rome's first emperor and was given the title Augustus.

CICERO (106–43BC)
Cicero is remembered as Rome's greatest orator, or speaker. Many of his letters and speeches still survive. He was a writer, poet, politican, lawyer and philosopher. He was elected consul of Rome in 63BC, but he had many enemies and was murdered in 43BC.

TIMELINE AD1–AD476

c.AD30 Death of Jesus Christ.

AD43 The Roman conquest of Britain begins.

Boudicca, queen of the Iceni in Britain

AD50 Rome is the largest city in the world – population about 1 million.

Roman traders reach Bengal and India.

AD60 Queen Boudicca leads an uprising in Britain.

AD64 The Great Fire of Rome.

AD75 Roman traders reach the Sudan, setting up trade links across the Sahara.

AD79 The volcano Vesuvius erupts, burying Pompeii and Herculaneum.

AD80 The Colosseum in Rome is completed.

Vesuvius begins to erupt

AD117 The Roman Empire is at its largest.

AD118-128 The Pantheon in Rome is built.

AD122 Construction work begins on Hadrian's Wall, a defensive barrier across northern Britain.

AD165-167 Plague spreads throughout the Empire.

the Pantheon in Rome

cAD200 Road system covers all parts of the Empire.

AD212 All free people in the Empire are granted citizenship.

AD1   AD50   AD100   AD150   AD200

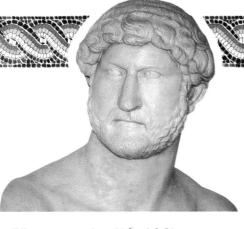

HADRIAN (AD76–138)

Hadrian became emperor in AD117 and spent many years travelling around the Empire. He had many splendid buildings constructed, as well as a defensive barrier across northern Britain, now known as Hadrian's Wall.

NERO (AD37–68) AND AGRIPPINA

Nero became emperor on the death of his adoptive father Claudius, in AD54. A cruel ruler, he was blamed for a great fire that destroyed much of Rome in AD64. Agrippina, his mother, was a powerful influence on him. She was suspected of poisoning two of her three husbands, and was eventually killed on her son's orders.

CLEOPATRA (68–30BC)

An Egyptian queen of Greek descent, Cleopatra had a son by Julius Caesar. She then fell in love with Mark Antony, a close follower of Caesar. They joined forces against Rome, but after a crushing defeat at Actium in 31BC, they both committed suicide. Egypt then became part of the Roman Empire.

JULIUS CAESAR (100–44BC)

Caesar was a talented and popular general and politician. He led Roman armies in an eight-year campaign to conquer Gaul (present-day France) in 50BC. In 49BC, he used his victorious troops to seize power and declare himself dictator for life. Five years later he was stabbed to death in the Senate by fellow politicians.

the cross, a symbol of Christianity

AD270 A new defensive wall is built around Rome by the Emperor Aurelian.

AD284 The Emperor Diocletian brings in new laws and taxes – divisions appear in the Empire.

AD313 Christianity is made legal in the Empire.

AD324 The Emperor Constantine reunites the Empire and founds the city of Constantinople (present-day Istanbul, in Turkey).

AD330 Constantine makes Constantinople his imperial residence and the new capital in the East.

AD395 The Roman Empire is divided again, this time into two parts – Eastern and Western.

the Emperor Constantine, depicted on a Roman coin

AD410 The city of Rome is raided and ransacked by Visigoth armies from Germany.

Vandal warrior

AD455 Vandal armies from Germany ransack Rome.

AD476 Fall of the Western Empire – the Eastern Empire survives until 1453.

D250   AD300   AD350   AD400   AD450

Rulers of Rome

IN THE EARLY DAYS, the city of Rome was ruled by kings. The first Roman king was said to be Romulus, the founder of the city in 753BC. The last king, a hated tyrant called Tarquinius the Proud, was thrown out in 509BC. The Romans then set up a republic. An assembly of powerful and wealthy citizens, the Senate, chose two consuls to lead them each year. By 493BC, the common people had their own representatives, too – the tribunes. In times of crisis, rulers could take on emergency powers and become dictators. The first Roman emperor, Augustus, was appointed by the Senate in 27BC. The emperors were given great powers and were even worshipped as gods. Some lived simply and ruled well, but others were violent, cruel men. They were surrounded by flatterers, and yet they lived in constant fear of plotters and murderers.

TRIUMPHAL PROCESSION
When a Roman general won a great victory, he was honoured with a military parade called a triumph. Cheering crowds lined the streets as the grand procession passed by. If a general was successful and popular, the way to power was often open to him. Probably the most famous Roman ruler of all, Julius Caesar, came to power after a series of brilliant military conquests.

STATE SACRIFICE
Roman emperors had religious as well as political duties. As *pontifex maximus*, or high priest, an emperor would make sacrifices as offerings to the gods at important festivals.

figs

DEADLY FRUIT

Who killed Augustus, the first Roman emperor, in AD14? It was hard to say. It might have been a natural death... but then again, it might have been caused by his wife Livia. She was said to have coated the figs in his garden with a deadly poison. Roman emperors were much feared, but they were surrounded by enemies and could trust no one, least of all their own families.

PRAETORIAN GUARDS

The Praetorian Guards were the emperor's personal bodyguards. They wore special uniforms and were well paid. The guards were the only armed soldiers allowed within the city of Rome and so became very powerful. They also intervened in politics – assassinating the Emperor Caligula and electing his successor, Claudius.

In Rome, wreaths made from leaves of the laurel tree were worn by emperors, victorious soldiers and athletes. The wreath was a badge of honour. The Romans copied the idea from the ancient Greeks.

WREATH OF HONOUR

You will need: tape measure, garden wire, pliers, scissors, clear tape, green ribbon, bay or laurel leaves (real or fake).

1 Measure around your head with the tape measure. Cut some wire the same length, so the wreath will fit you. Bend the wire as shown and tape the ribbon round it.

2 Start to tape the leaves by their stems on to the wire, as shown above. Work your way around to the middle of the wire, fanning out the leaves as you go.

3 Then reverse the direction of the leaves and work your way around the rest of the wire. Fit the finished wreath to your head. Hail, Caesar!

Roman Society

Roman society was never very fair. At first, a group of rich and powerful noble families, called the patricians, controlled the city and the Senate. Anyone who wanted their voice heard had to persuade a senator to speak on their behalf. Over the centuries the common citizens, known as plebeians, became more powerful until, by 287BC, they shared equally in government. Eventually, in the days of the Empire, even people of humble birth could become emperor, provided they were wealthy or had the support of the army. Emperors always feared riots by the common people of Rome, so they tried to keep the people happy with handouts of free food and lavish entertainments. Roman women had little power outside the family and could not vote. However, many were successful in business or had an important influence on political events. Slaves had very few rights, though Roman society depended on slave labour. Prisoners of war were bought and sold as slaves and many were treated cruelly, making slave revolts common.

A Roman Consul

This is a statue of a Roman consul, or leader of the Senate, in the days of the republic. At first, only the noble, and often wealthy, ruling class could be senators. However, under the emperors, the power and influence of the Senate slowly grew less and less.

Life as a Slave

The everyday running of the Empire depended on slavery. This mosaic shows a young slave boy carrying fruit. In about AD100, a wealthy family might have had as many as 500 slaves. Some families treated their slaves well, and slaves who gave good service might earn their freedom. However, many more led miserable lives, toiling in the mines or labouring in the fields.

Slave Tag

This bronze disc was probably worn around the neck of a slave, like a dog-tag. The Latin words on it say: "Hold me, in case I run away, and return me to my master Viventius on the estate of Callistus". Slaves had few rights and could be branded on the forehead or leg as the property of their owners.

COLLECTING TAXES

This stone carving probably shows people paying their annual taxes. Officials counted the population of the Empire and registered them for paying tax. Money from taxes paid for the army and the government. However, many of the tax collectors took bribes, and even emperors seized public money to add to their private fortunes.

ARISTOCRATS

This Italian painting of the 1700s imagines how a noble Roman lady might dress after bathing. Wealthy people had personal slaves to help them bathe, dress and look after their hair. Household slaves were sometimes almost part of the family, and their children might be brought up and educated with their owner's children.

Living in the Country

THE FIRST ROMANS mostly lived by farming. Even when Rome had become a big city, Roman poets still liked to sing the praises of the countryside. In reality, country life was quite hard. Oxen were used for ploughing. Grain crops were harvested with a sickle, and flour was often ground by hand. Water had to be fetched by hand from the farm's well or a nearby spring.

Many farms were very small. They were often run by retired soldiers, who would raise chickens and geese and perhaps a cow or pig. They would also keep bees and grow olives and a few vegetables.

Other farms in Italy and across the Empire were large estates set up to provide incomes for their wealthy landowners. These estates might have their own olive presses, reaping machines and stores for drying grain. An estate was often laid out around a large, luxurious house or villa. Other villas were grand country houses owned by rich and powerful Romans.

A COUNTRY ESTATE
Life on a country estate was always busy, as this mosaic of a Roman villa in Tunisia, North Africa, shows. North African country estates supplied Rome with vast amounts of grain, fruit and vegetables. The good soil, combined with hot summers and rain in winter, made farming easy.

HADRIAN'S VILLA
One of the grandest country houses of all was built for the Emperor Hadrian between AD124 and 133. Parts of the villa still stand today, as this view of one of its lakeside walks shows. The luxurious villa itself stood on a hilltop, with Rome just visible in the distance. Built on land that belonged to Hadrian's family, the villa had pavilions and pools, terraces, banqueting halls, theatres and libraries. All around the villa were parklands filled with trees, such as laurels, planes and pines, exotic shrubs and formal flowerbeds. Hadrian designed the villa as a holiday palace where he could escape from the cares of government, but he died just four years after it was completed.

FOOD FOR ROME

Rome needed huge amounts of food for all its people. Vegetables, such as leeks, celery, cabbage, beans and peas, were grown at market gardens around the city. Grain crops included wheat, barley, oats and rye. Grapes were made into wine and, as there was no sugar, honey was used to sweeten foods.

grapes

wheat

honey

HUNTING WILD BOAR

Hunting scenes often decorated the walls of country villas. The hunt was a favourite pastime for young noblemen or army officers visiting the countryside. A wild boar, like the one shown in this mosaic, was one of the most dangerous animals of all when it charged.

GROVES OF OLIVE TREES

Olives were, and still are, an important crop in the lands around the Mediterranean. They were grown on small farms as well as on large estates. The oil was pressed and stored in large pottery jars. It was used for cooking or burnt in oil lamps.

PLOUGHING THE LAND

This ploughman from Roman Britain is using a heavy wooden plough drawn by oxen. Large areas of Europe were still covered in thick forest in the days of the Roman Empire. Gradually farmers cleared land to plough, and farmland and orchards spread across the countryside.

Town and City

MANY OF THE TOWNS in Italy and the lands surrounding the Mediterranean Sea were already old and well-established when the Romans invaded. Under Roman rule these towns prospered and grew. In other parts of Europe, where people had never lived in a big town, the Roman invaders built impressive new cities.

Roman towns had straight, paved roads planned on a grid pattern. Some were broad streets with pavements. Others were alleys just wide enough for a donkey. Most streets were busy with noisy crowds, street merchants, carts and rowdy bars. The streets divided the buildings into blocks called *insulae*, which means islands. The homes of wealthy families were spacious and comfortable. Poorer Romans often lived in apartment blocks that were badly built, crowded and in constant danger of burning down.

Fresh water was brought into towns through a system of channels called an aqueduct. The water was piped to fountains, public baths and to the homes of the wealthy.

THE STREETS OF POMPEII
On August 24, AD79, the volcano Vesuvius erupted violently, burying the Roman town of Pompeii in ash and lava. Work began in 1748 to excavate the ancient town, and its streets, shops and houses have slowly been revealed. In this excavated street, the deep ruts in the road made by cart wheels are clearly visible. Streets were often filled with mud and filth, so stepping-stones were laid for pedestrians to cross.

AN AQUEDUCT BRIDGE

You will need: ruler, pencil, scissors, thick and thin card, PVA glue, paintbrush, masking tape, modelling clay, plaster paste, acrylic paints, water pot.

37cm
3.5cm
40.5cm
10.5cm
7.5cm   2.5cm   1.5cm
41.5cm
10.5cm
7.5cm   2.5cm   2cm

Cut out pieces of card following the measurements shown.

1 Draw and cut out the shapes of the arches from the thick card. You need to cut out a pair for each level of the aqueduct – top, middle and bottom.

78

AQUEDUCTS

Water was carried into Roman towns and cities through a system of channels and pipes called aqueducts. Most of these were underground. Sometimes they were supported on high arches, such as this one, which still stands today in France. The water came from fresh springs, streams and lakes.

HERCULANEUM

The volcanic eruption that buried Pompeii caused a mud flow that buried a nearby coastal town, Herculaneum. Here, too, archaeologists have discovered houses, public baths, shops and workshops side by side on the city's streets. This view shows how crowded parts of the town were, with narrow paved streets separating the buildings.

CITY PLAN

This aerial view of Pompeii clearly shows how Roman streets were laid out on a grid pattern.

Forum baths

Stabian baths

amphitheatre

sports ground

N

large theatre

market

Forum

Capitol

| 0 | 200 | 400m |
| 0 | 200 | 400yds |

Aqueducts were built at a slight slope to ensure a steady flow of water. Arched bridges carried them across river valleys. The water flowed along a channel at the top of the bridge.

2 Cut strips of thin card in three widths – 4cm, 2.5cm and 2cm. These are for the insides of the arches. Use glue and tape to fix the 4cm strips to the bottom level.

3 Glue on the other side of the bottom level. Fix it securely with tape. Cut a top section from thick card and fix this on. Make the two other levels in the same way.

4 Roll the modelling clay into buttresses and wrap with thick card. Attach these to the three central arches of the bottom level. These will support the aqueduct bridge.

5 Glue the levels together. Cover the model with plaster paste and mark on a brick pattern. Leave to dry. Paint the arches grey. Paint a blue channel of 'water' on top.

House and Garden

ONLY WEALTHY ROMANS could afford to live in a private house. A typical town house was designed to look inwards, with the rooms arranged round a central courtyard and a walled garden. Outside walls had few windows and these were small and shuttered. The front door opened on to a short passage leading into an airy courtyard called an *atrium*. Front rooms on either side of the passage were usually used as bedrooms. Sometimes they were used as workshops or shops, having shutters that opened out to the street.

The centre of the atrium was open to the sky. Below this opening was a pool, set into the floor, to collect rainwater. Around the atrium were more bedrooms and the kitchen. If you were a guest or had important business you would be shown into the *tablinium*. The dining room, or *triclinium*, was often the grandest room of all. The very rich sometimes also had a summer dining room, which looked on to the garden.

Houses were made of locally available building materials. These might include stone, mud bricks, cement and timber. Roofs were made of clay tiles.

garden

bedroom

tablinium (living room and office)

LOCKS AND KEYS
This was the key to the door of a Roman house. Pushed in through a keyhole, the prongs at the end of the key fitted into holes in the bolt in the lock. The key could then be used to slide the bolt along and unlock the door.

INSIDE A ROMAN HOME
The outside of a wealthy Roman's town house was usually quite plain, but inside it was highly decorated with elaborate wall paintings and intricate mosaics. The rooms were sparsely furnished, with couches or beds, small side tables, benches and folding stools. There were few windows, but high ceilings and wide doors made the most of the light from the open atrium and the garden.

MAKE A ROMAN HOME
You will need: pencil, ruler, thick card, scissors, PVA glue, paintbrushes, masking tape, corrugated cardboard, thin card, water pot, acrylic paints.

Cut out pieces of card following the measurements shown.

water spout

atrium
(courtyard)

bedroom

triclinium
(dining room)

kitchen

At the back of many Roman houses lay beautiful, walled gardens with stone columns, pools, fountains, statues and terraces. People would eat out here on warm evenings, reclining on couches and surrounded by trailing ivy, sweet-smelling roses, irises, lilies, bay trees and cypresses.

ivy

roses

This Roman house has high, windowless walls to shut out the hot summer sun, making it cool and shady inside.

1 Cut out the pieces of thick card. Edge each piece with glue. Press the pieces together and reinforce with masking tape, as shown. You have now made the walls of your house.

2 Measure your model and cut out pieces of corrugated cardboard for the roofs. Stick them together with glue, as shown above. Paint the roofs red.

3 Rainwater running down the sloped atrium roof was directed into a pool below by gutters and water spouts. Make gutters from strips of thin card, with holes as spouts.

4 Paint the house walls as shown, using masking tape to get a straight line. Glue on the roofs. Why not finish off your Roman house with some authentic graffiti!

81

In the Kitchen

When a large meal was being prepared, slaves would have to carry water and fresh kindling for the fire into the kitchen. As the fires were lit, the room would become quite smoky because there was no chimney. Soon the coals would be glowing red hot and pots would be boiling on trivets and griddles on the raised brick stove. Food was boiled, fried, grilled and stewed. Larger kitchens might include stone ovens for baking bread or spits for roasting meat. A few even had piped hot water.

The kitchens of wealthy Romans were well equipped with all kinds of bronze pots, pans, strainers and ladles. Pottery storage jars held wine, olive oil and sauces. Herbs, vegetables and joints of meat hung from hooks in the roof. There were no tins, and no fridges or freezers to keep food fresh. Food had to be preserved in oil or by drying, smoking, salting or pickling.

mortar

Valuable Glass

This glass bottle or jug was made about 1,900 years ago. Precious liquids or expensive perfumes were sold in bottles like this throughout the Empire. When a bottle was empty, it was far too valuable to throw away, so it was often reused to store food such as honey in the kitchen.

Pestle and Mortar

The Romans liked spicy food. Roman cooks used a pestle and mortar to grind up foods, such as nuts, herbs and spices, into a paste. Both pieces were usually made of a very tough pottery or stone. The rough inside of the mortar was made of coarse grit to help grind the food.

pestle

A Roman Kitchen

You will need: pencil, ruler, cardboard, scissors, paintbrush, PVA glue, masking tape, water pot, acrylic paints, red felt tip pen, plaster paste, balsa wood, sandpaper, self-drying clay, work board, modelling tool.

1 Cut out the walls and floor of the kitchen from cardboard, as shown. Glue the edges and press them together. Reinforce the walls with pieces of masking tape.

2 Paint the floor grey. When dry, use the ruler and pencil to draw on stone flags. Paint the walls yellow, edged with blue. When dry, use the felt tip to draw stripes.

3 Cut out pieces of card to make a stove about 2cm long, 5cm wide and 4cm high. Glue the pieces together and reinforce with masking tape, as shown above.

READY FOR THE COOK

Herbs brought fresh from the garden included coriander, oregano, rue, mint, thyme and parsley. Food was spiced with pepper, caraway, aniseed, mustard seeds and saffron. On the table there might be eggs, grapes, figs and nuts. Much of our knowledge of Roman cooking comes from recipes collected by a Roman gourmet called Apicius nearly 2,000 years ago.

saffron

thyme

mint

quails' eggs

BAKING PAN

This bronze tray was probably used as a mould for baking honey cakes, buns or pastries. The long handle makes it easier to remove from a hot oven. It may also have been used to cook eggs.

STRAINER

This bronze strainer was used by Roman cooks to strain sauces. It was made using the same design as a saucepan, but its bowl has been pierced with an intricate pattern. The hole in the handle was used to hang it from a hook on the wall.

SAUCEPAN

Like many Roman kitchen utensils, this saucepan is made from bronze. Bronze contains copper, which can give food a very strange flavour – the inside of the saucepan has been coated with silver to prevent this from happening.

Foods in a Roman kitchen were stored in baskets, bowls or sacks. Wine, oil and sauces were stored in pottery jars called amphorae.

4 Coat the stove with plaster paste. Leave to dry. Then use sandpaper to rub it smooth. Make a grate from two strips of card and four bits of balsa wood, glued together.

5 Use the acrylic paints to colour the stove and the grate, as shown above. Use small pieces of balsa wood to make a pile of wood fuel to store underneath the stove.

6 Make a table and shelves from balsa wood, as shown. Glue them together, and bind with masking tape. Leave them to dry before painting the pieces brown.

7 Use the clay to model pots, pans, bowls, storage jars, perhaps even a frying pan or an egg poacher. Leave the utensils to dry before painting them a suitable colour.

Good Eating

For poor Romans, a meal was often little more than a hurried bowl of porridge or a crust of bread washed down with sour wine. Many town-dwellers lived in homes without kitchens. They ate takeaway meals bought from the many food stalls and bars in town. Even for wealthier people, breakfast might be just a quick snack of bread, honey and olives. Lunch, too, was a light meal, perhaps of eggs or cold meats and fruit. The main meal of the day was *cena*, or dinner. This evening meal might start with shellfish or a salad, followed by a main course of roast meat, such as pork, veal, chicken or goose, with vegetables. It finished with a sweet course of fruit or honey cakes.

More lavish banquets might include fattened dormice, songbirds, flamingoes' tongues or a custard made from calves' brains and rose hips! Food was heavily spiced and was often served with a fish sauce called *garum*. Wine was usually mixed with water and sometimes flavoured with honey or spices. Guests could take home any tasty morsels that were left over.

Serving Slaves
This mosaic shows a slave called Paregorius helping to prepare his master's table for a banquet. On his head he is carrying a tray with plates of food. During a banquet, dishes were brought in a few at a time and set down on a small table. All the food was cooked and served by slaves.

Honeyed Dates

You will need: chopping board, dates, small knife, walnuts, pecan nuts, almonds, hazelnuts, pestle and mortar, salt, 175ml honey, frying pan, wooden spoon, a few fresh mint leaves.

1 On the chopping board, slit open the dates with the knife. Remove the stone inside. Be sure not to cut the dates completely in half and be careful with the knife.

2 Put aside the hazelnuts. Chop up the rest of the nuts. Use a pestle and mortar to grind them into smaller pieces. Stuff a small amount into the middle of each date.

3 Pour some salt on to the chopping board and lightly roll each date in it. Make sure the dates are coated all over, but do not use too much salt.

CUPS

Pottery cups like this one were used for drinking wine. Many drinking cups had handles and were often highly decorated. Metal cups could make wine taste unpleasant, so coloured glass cups and pottery cups were more popular.

THE FAMILY SILVER

These silver spoons were used by a wealthy family in Roman Britain. Food was usually eaten with the fingers, but spoons were used for sauces. At banquets, Romans liked to bring out their best silver tableware as a sign of status.

AT A BANQUET

This wall painting shows a typical Roman banquet. Guests usually sat three to a couch. After the meal they were entertained with poetry readings and music, or jokes and jugglers. Dress and table manners were very important at a banquet. Arguments and bad language were not allowed, but it was fine to spit, belch or even eat until you were sick!

4 On a low heat, melt the honey in the frying pan. Lightly fry the dates for five minutes, turning them with a wooden spoon. Take care while using the stove.

5 Arrange the stuffed dates in a shallow dish. Sprinkle over the whole hazelnuts, some chopped nuts and a few leaves of fresh mint. Now they are ready to serve to your friends.

The Romans loved sweet dishes made from nuts and dates imported from North Africa. They also used dates to make sauces for savoury dishes such as fish and roast duck.

Getting Dressed

MOST ROMAN CLOTHES were made of wool that had been spun and woven by hand at home or in a workshop. Flax was grown in Egypt to make linen, while cotton from India and silk from China were rare and expensive imports. The most common style of clothing was a simple tunic, which was practical for people who led active lives, such as workers, slaves and children. Important men also wore a white robe called a toga. This was a 6m length of cloth with a curved edge, wrapped around the body and draped over the shoulder. It was heavy and uncomfortable to wear, but looked very impressive. Women wore a long dress called a *stola*, over an under-tunic. Often they also wore a *palla* – a large shawl that could be arranged in various ways. Girls wore white until they were married, after which they often wore dresses dyed in bright colours.

ROMAN FOOTWEAR
This sandal (*left*) and child's shoe (*far left*) were found in York, in Britain. Most Romans wore open leather sandals. There were many different designs, and some had nailed soles to make them harder wearing. Shoes and boots were worn in the colder parts of the Empire.

DRESSING FOR DIONYSUS
Wall paintings in the homes of wealthy Romans hold many clues about the way people dressed in the Roman world. This scene was found in the Villa of the Mysteries, in Pompeii. It shows young women being prepared as ceremonial brides for Dionysus, the god of wine.

WEAR A TOGA

You will need: old white sheet, tape measure, scissors for cutting cloth and scissors for sticky tape, double-sided sticky tape, purple ribbon, long T-shirt, cord.

1 Ask a friend to help you with the toga. They can pretend to be your slave – wealthy Romans had slaves to help them dress. Fold the sheet in half along its length. Cut the ends to make rounded corners at each end, as shown. Use double-sided tape to stick the ribbon along the long edge. Put on a long white T-shirt tied at the waist with cord.

2 This is a simple way to put on a toga. Get your friend to hold the long, straight edge of fabric behind you. Drape about a quarter of the toga over your left arm and shoulder.

WORKERS' CLOTHES

Not all Romans wore flowing robes. This man is probably a farm worker from Roman Germany. He wears strips of cloth around his legs and a hooded leather cloak to protect him from the cold, wet weather. Hooded cloaks like this were exported from Gaul (present-day France) and Britain.

DRESSED TO IMPRESS

This stone carving shows the family of the Emperor Augustus, dressed for an important state occasion. The women are all shown wearing a *stola*, with a *palla* draped round their shoulders or head. The men and boys are shown in togas. A toga could be worn by all free Roman citizens, but only the wealthy upper classes wore it. This was because it took time – and a helping hand – to put on a toga. Once you had it on, it was also quite awkward to move in!

3 Bring the rest of the toga round to the front, passing it under your right arm. Hook the toga up by tucking a few folds of material securely into the cord around your waist.

4 Now your friend can help you fold the rest of the toga neatly over your left arm, as shown above. If you prefer, you could drape it all over your left shoulder.

Boys from wealthy families wore togas edged with a thin purple stripe until they reached the age of 16. They then wore plain togas. A toga with a broad purple stripe was worn by Roman senators. Purple dye was expensive, so the colour was only worn by high-ranking citizens.

Fashion and Beauty

A ROMAN LADY would spend most of the morning surrounded by her female slaves. Some would bring her a mirror made of bronze or silver and jars of perfumed oils or ointments. Another slave would comb out her hair – and could expect a spiteful jab with a hairpin if she pulled at a tangle.

Most rich women wanted to look pale – after all, only women who had to work outdoors became sunburnt. So chalk, or even a poisonous powder made from white lead, was rubbed into the face. Face packs were made of bread and milk. One remedy for spots and pimples included bird droppings! Lipsticks and blusher were made of red ochre or the sediment from red wine. Eyeshadow was made of ash and saffron. Women's hair was curled, plaited or pinned up, according to the latest fashion.

PORTRAIT OF A LADY
This is a portrait of a lady who lived in the Roman province of Egypt. Her earrings and necklace are made of emeralds, garnets and pearls set in gold. They are a sign of her wealth as they would have been very expensive. Her hair has been curled, and lamp-black or soot may have been used to darken her eyelashes and eyebrows.

CARVED COMB
This comb is carved from ivory and is inscribed in Latin with the words "Modestina farewell". Combs of silver and ivory were used to decorate the intricate hairstyles favoured by many Roman women. The poor used wooden or bone combs, though more out of need than fashion.

SCENT BOTTLES
These lovely perfume bottles belonged to a Roman lady. The round one is made of hand-blown, gold-banded glass. The other is carved from onyx, a precious stone with layers of different colours.

A GOLDEN HEADDRESS
You will need: tape measure, plain card, pencil, scissors, PVA glue, paintbrush, string, plastic beads, gold foil wrappers, sticky tape or paper clip.

1 Measure around your head with the tape measure. Draw the shape of the tiara to the same length on card. Also draw outlines for various sizes of leaf shape, as shown.

2 Carefully cut out the tiara outline from the card. Also cut out the leaf shapes. Then cut out the centre of each one so that they look a bit like arches.

3 Use the PVA glue and a paintbrush to paste the shapes securely on to the front of the tiara. These will be part of an elegant pattern for your tiara.

CROWNING GLORY

This lady's elaborately curled hair is almost certainly a wig. Hairpieces and wigs were always popular with wealthy Roman women– a bride would wear at least six pads of artificial hair at her wedding. Locks of black hair were usually imported from Asia, while blond or red hair came from northern Europe.

MEN'S CHANGING HAIRSTYLES

Roman men were just as concerned with their appearance as women. They usually wore their hair short, either combed forward or curled. They were mostly clean shaven, but beards became fashionable during the reign of the Emperor Hadrian, AD117–138.

A FINE DISPLAY

This picture shows a ceremonial dance at the Temple of the Sun in Rome. Both the men and women are wearing golden headdresses decorated with precious jewels and gold filigree. Lavish displays like this were reserved for grand public occasions to show off the wealth and power of the Empire.

RINGS ON THEIR FINGERS

Both men and women wore jewellery, especially rings. Rich people would wear rings like these, usually made of gold or silver. Emeralds, pearls and amber were also used in rings. The less wealthy would wear rings of bronze.

4 Cut lengths of string and glue them around the inside edges of the shapes. Glue plastic beads at the top of each arch, so that they look like precious stones.

5 Collect gold foil from sweet wrappers and glue it on to the tiara. Use the end of the paintbrush to carefully poke the foil into all the corners around the beads.

The finished tiara can be held together at the back by tape or a clip. Roman ladies liked to wear tiaras made of gold, with jewels in their hair.

Lessons and Learning

MOST CHILDREN in the Roman Empire never went to school. They learned a trade from their parents or found out about sums by trading on a market stall. Boys might be trained to fight with swords or to ride horses, in preparation for joining the army. Girls would be taught how to run the home, in preparation for marriage.

Wealthy families did provide an education for their sons and sometimes for their daughters, too. They were usually taught at home by a private tutor, but there were also small schools. Tutors and schoolmasters would teach children arithmetic, and how to read and write in both Latin and Greek. Clever pupils might also learn public speaking skills, poetry and history. Girls often had music lessons at home, on a harp-like instrument called a lyre.

INKPOTS AND PENS
Pen and ink were used to write on scrolls made from papyrus (a kind of reed) or thin sheets of wood. Ink was often made from soot or lamp-black, mixed with water. It was kept in inkpots such as these. Inkpots were made from glass, pottery or metal. Pens were made from bone, reeds or bronze.

WRITING IN WAX
This painting shows a couple from Pompeii. The man holds a parchment scroll. His wife is probably going through their household accounts. She holds a wax-covered writing tablet and a stylus to scratch words into the wax. A stylus had a pointed end for writing and a flat end for rubbing out.

A WRITING TABLET

You will need: sheets and sticks of balsa wood, craft knife, ruler, PVA glue, paintbrush, brown acrylic paint, water pot, modelling clay, work board, rolling pin, modelling tool, skewer, purple thread, pencil (to be used as a stylus), gold paint.

1 Use the craft knife to cut the balsa sheet into two rectangles 10cm x 22cm. The sticks of balsa should be cut into four lengths 22cm long and four lengths 10cm long.

2 Glue the sticks around the edges of each sheet as shown. These form a shallow hollow into which you can press the 'wax'. Paint the two frames a rich brown colour.

3 Roll out the modelling clay on a board and place a balsa frame on top. Use the modelling tool to cut around the outside of the frame. Repeat this step.

TEACHER AND PUPILS
This stone sculpture from Roman Germany shows a teacher seated between two of his pupils. They are reading their lessons from papyrus scrolls. Children had to learn poetry and other writings by heart. Any bad behaviour or mistakes were punished with a beating.

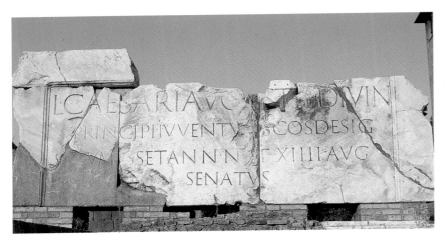

WRITING IT DOWN
Various materials were used for writing. Melted beeswax was poured into wooden trays to make writing tablets. Letters were scratched into the wax, which could be used again and again. Powdered soot was mixed with water and other ingredients to make ink for writing on papyrus, parchment or wood.

soot

melted beeswax

Roman numerals on papyrus

LETTERS IN STONE
Temples, monuments and public buildings were covered in Latin inscriptions, such as this one. Each letter was beautifully chiselled by a stonemason. These words are carved in marble. The inscription marked the 14th birthday of Lucius Caesar, the grandson of the Emperor Augustus.

4 Cut off about 1cm all around the edge of each modelling clay rectangle. This helps to make sure that the modelling clay will fit inside the balsa wood frame.

5 Carefully press the clay into each side – this represents the wax. Use the skewer to poke two holes through the inside edge of each frame, as shown.

6 Join the two frames together by threading purple thread through each pair of holes and tying it securely together. You have now made your tablet.

Paint the pencil gold to make it look as if it is made of metal. Use it like a stylus to scratch words on your tablet. Why not try writing in Latin? You could write CIVIS ROMANVS SVM, which means "I am a Roman citizen".

In the Forum

EVERY LARGE ROMAN TOWN had a forum – a market square with public buildings around it. This was where people gathered to do business and exchange friendly gossip. In the morning, while the lady of the house had her hair done and her children struggled with their lessons, her husband would walk over to the forum.

In the forum's central square, crowds thronged around market stalls. Sometimes a public row might break out as inspectors of weights and measures accused some trader of cheating his customers. Around the square were shops, imposing monuments, marble statues and temples to the gods. The walls of buildings were often scrawled with graffiti made up of political messages, personal insults or declarations of love. On one side of the forum was the basilica, a large building used as the town hall, a law court and public meeting place. Some of the crowds may have been members of the *curia* or town council, or one of the trade guilds who had their halls there.

DOWNTOWN POMPEII
The ruins at Pompeii include these remains of a row of columns. They were part of a two-storey colonnade that once took up three sides of the forum. Rows of shops and market stalls were set up behind the colonnade at ground level.

TEMPLES AND PROSPERITY
The forum of every town had splendid temples to the many gods and goddesses of ancient Rome. There were also temples for famous Romans. The grand columns of this temple still remain in the forum at Rome. Today, a Christian church stands behind it. The temple was built in honour of Antoninus Pius, one of Rome's wisest emperors, and his wife Faustina.

MAKING MONEY

Money changers and bankers gathered to make deals and discuss business in the forum. Here, too, tax collectors raised money for the town council – taxes were charged on all goods that passed through the town.

FAST FOOD

As people hurried to work or chatted with friends, they might pick up a snack from a food stall or a street vendor. Pastries filled with spicy meats made popular snacks. On market day, the forum would also be busy with traders and farmers setting up stalls in the central square.

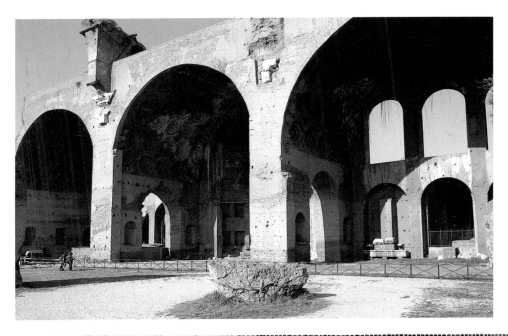

THE BASILICA

This is the Basilica of Maxentius in Rome. A basilica was a huge building used as a cross between a town hall and law courts. It usually had a very high roof, supported by rows of columns. The columns divided the building into a central area with two side aisles. People came here to work, do business or simply chat with friends.

Shopping – Roman Style

IN MOST LARGE TOWNS, shops spread out from the forum and along the main streets. Shops were usually small, family-run businesses. At the start of the working day, shutters or blinds would be taken from the shop front and goods put on display. Noise would soon fill the air as bakers, butchers, fishmongers, fruit and vegetable sellers all began crying out that their produce was the best and cheapest. Joints of meat might be hung from a pole, while ready-cooked food, grains or oils would be sold from pots set into a stone counter. Other shops sold pottery lamps or bronze lanterns, kitchen pots and pans or knives, while some traders repaired shoes or laundered cloth. Hammering and banging coming from the workshops at the back added to the clamour of a busy main street.

ROMAN MONEY
The same currency was used throughout the Roman Empire. Coins were made of gold, silver and bronze. Shoppers kept their money in purses made of cloth or leather or in wooden boxes.

GOING TO MARKET
This is a view of Trajan's Market, which was a five-storey group of shops set into a hillside in Rome. Most Roman towns had covered halls or central markets like this, where shops were rented out to traders.

A ROMAN DELICATESSEN
About 1,700 years ago this was the place to buy good food in Ostia, the seaport nearest to Rome. Bars, inns and cafés were fitted with stone counters that were often decorated with coloured marble. At lunchtime, bars like this would be busy with customers enjoying a meal.

A BUTCHER'S SHOP
A Roman butcher uses a cleaver to prepare chops while a customer waits for her order. Butchers' shops have changed very little over the ages – pork, lamb and beef were sold, and sausages were popular, too. On the right hangs a steelyard, a metal bar with a pan like a scale, for weighing the meat.

DISHING IT UP
These are the remains of a shop that sold food. Set into the marble counter are big pottery containers, called *dolia*. These were used for displaying and serving up food, such as beans and lentils. They were also used for keeping jars of wine cool on hot summer days. The containers could be covered with wooden or stone lids to keep out the flies.

Trades and Crafts

THERE WERE POTTERY WORKSHOPS throughout the Roman Empire. Clay pots were made by turning and shaping wet clay on a wheel and baking it in a kiln. Some of the best clay came from the district of Arretium, in Italy. Large pottery centres in Gaul (present-day France) produced a very popular red pottery called Samian ware. In Roman Germany, pottery drinking cups were coloured black and decorated in white with mottoes such as "Drink Up!" or "Bring Me Wine!" – in Latin, of course!

The Romans learned from the Syrians how to blow glass into shapes on the end of a long tube. This was a new and simple technique, although ways of making glass had been known for centuries. As a result, glass became widely used in Roman times.

The skills of the blacksmith were called for everyday, all over the Empire. Smiths hammered away on their anvils, shaping iron tools, weapons and pots. Some metalworkers were fine artists, working in gold, silver and bronze.

THE BLACKSMITHS' GOD
The Romans believed in many different gods. This is a statue of Vulcan, the god of smiths, or metalworkers. He is holding a hammer, used to shape hot metal on an anvil.

COPPERSMITHS
A typical busy day at a coppersmiths' workshop. A customer and his son look on as one of the smiths hammers out sheets of hot copper on an anvil. Another smith is bent over his work, decorating a copper bowl. The goods they are selling are displayed on the wall and hung from the ceiling.

SAMIAN POTTERY
This decorated bowl was found at Felixstowe, in Britain. Glossy red Samian ware was made in Gaul (present-day France), in workshops almost as big as factories. This popular pottery was transported all over the Empire, by land and by sea.

ROMAN SHOP
This stone carving shows a Roman shop with cloth and cushions for sale. Customers are seated while the shopkeeper shows them his wares. The Romans were skilled sculptors and much of our knowledge about the Empire comes from detailed carvings in stone such as this one.

NATURAL DYES
Roman textile workers used a variety of natural dyes on cloth, including onion skins (a golden yellow dye), pine cones (a reddish-yellow dye) and tree bark (a reddish-brown dye). Other natural sources included berries, leaves, minerals, shellfish, nettles and saffron from crocuses.

ROMAN GLASSMAKING
Quality glass was made into bowls, jugs, flasks and bottles. Some were very simple in design, while others were highly decorated. Bands of coloured glass and even gold were used in some pieces. The finest glassware was used by wealthy Romans, and was always brought out when they entertained guests.

bark

fir cones

onion

Pictures and Statues

THE ROMANS loved to decorate their homes and public places with paintings and statues. Mosaics were pictures made using *tesserae* – cubes of stone, pottery or glass – which were pressed into soft cement. Mosaic pictures might show hunting scenes, the harvest or Roman gods. Geometric patterns were popular and often used as borders.

Wall paintings, or murals, often showed garden scenes, birds and animals or heroes and goddesses. They were painted on to wooden panels or directly on to the wall. Roman artists loved to trick the eye by painting false columns, archways and shelves. The Romans were skilled sculptors, using stone, marble and bronze. They imitated the ancient Greeks in putting up marble statues in public places and gardens. These might be of gods and goddesses or emperors and generals.

A COUNTRY SCENE
This man and wild boar are part of a mosaic made in Roman North Africa. Making a mosaic was quite tricky – rather like doing a jigsaw puzzle. Even so, skilled artists could create lifelike scenes from cubes of coloured glass, pottery and stone.

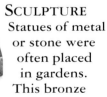

SCULPTURE
Statues of metal or stone were often placed in gardens. This bronze figure is in the remains of a house in Pompeii. It is of a faun, a god of the countryside.

FLOOR MOSAICS
Birds, animals, plants and country scenes were popular subjects for mosaics. These parrots are part of a much larger, and quite elaborate, floor mosaic from a Roman house.

MAKE A MOSAIC

You will need: rough paper, pencil, ruler, scissors, large sheet of card, self-drying clay, rolling pin, wooden board, modelling knife, acrylic paints, paintbrush, water pot, clear varnish and brush (optional), plaster paste, spreader, muslin rag.

1 Sketch out your mosaic design on rough paper. A simple design like this one is good to start with. Cut the card so it measures 25cm x 10cm. Copy the design on to it.

2 Roll out the clay on the board. Use the ruler to measure out small squares on the clay. Cut them out with the modelling knife. Leave to dry. These will be your tesserae.

3 Paint the pieces in batches of different colours, as shown above. When the paint is dry, you can coat them with clear varnish for extra strength and shine. Leave to dry.

MOSAIC MATERIALS

Mosaics were often made inside frames, in workshops, and then transported to where they were to be used. Sometimes, the tesserae were brought to the site and fitted on the spot by the workers. The floor of an average room in a Roman town house might need over 100,000 pieces.

tesserae

pot shards

MUSICIANS AND DANCERS

This dramatic painting is on the walls of an excavated villa in Pompeii. It is one in a series of paintings that show the secret rites, or mysteries, honouring the god Dionysus.

REAL OR FAKE?

Roman artists liked to make painted objects appear real enough to touch. This bowl of fruit on a shelf is typical of this style of painting. It was found on the wall of a villa that belonged to a wealthy Roman landowner.

4 Spread the plaster paste on to the card, a small part at a time. While it is still wet, press in your tesserae following the design, as shown. Use your sketch as an extra guide.

5 When the mosaic is dry, use the muslin rag to polish up the surface. Any other soft, dry cloth would also be suitable. Now your mosaic is ready for display.

The Romans liked to have mosaics in their homes. Wealthy people often had elaborate mosaics in their courtyards and dining rooms, as these were rooms that visitors would see.

Doctors and Medicine

SOME ROMANS lived to a ripe old age, but most died before they reached the age of 50. Archaeologists have found out a lot about health and disease in Roman times by examining skeletons that have survived. They can tell, for example, how old a person was when they died and their general state of health during their life. Ancient writings also provide information about Roman medical knowledge.

Roman doctors knew very little science. They healed the sick through a mixture of common sense, trust in the gods and magic. Most cures and treatments had come to Rome from the doctors of ancient Greece. The Greeks and Romans also shared the same god of healing, Aesculapius. There were doctors in most parts of the Empire, as well as midwives, dentists and eye specialists. Surgeons operated on wounds received in battle, on broken bones and even skulls.

The only pain killers were made from poppy juice – an operation must have been a terrible ordeal.

GODDESS OF HEALTH
Greeks and Romans honoured the daughter of the god Aesculapius as a goddess of health. She was called Hygieia. The word hygienic, which comes from her name, is still used today to mean free of germs.

A CHEMIST'S SHOP
This pharmacy, or chemist's shop, is run by a woman. This was quite unusual for Roman times, as women were rarely given positions of responsibility. Roman pharmacists collected herbs and often mixed them for doctors.

MEDICINE BOX
Boxes like this one would have been used by Roman doctors to store various drugs. Many of the treatments used by doctors were herbal, and not always pleasant to take!

MEDICAL INSTRUMENTS
The Romans used a variety of surgical and other instruments. These are made in bronze and include a scalpel, forceps and a spatula for mixing and applying various ointments.

TAKING THE CURE

These are the ruins of a medical clinic in Asia Minor (present-day Turkey). It was built around AD150, in honour of Aesculapius, the god of healing. Clinics like this one were known as therapy buildings. People would come to them seeking cures for all kinds of ailments.

BATHING THE BABY

This stone carving from Rome shows a newborn baby being bathed. The Romans were well aware of the importance of regular bathing in clean water. However, childbirth itself was dangerous for both mother and baby. Despite the dangers, the Romans liked to have large families, and many women died giving birth.

HERBAL MEDICINE

Doctors and travelling healers sold all kinds of potions and ointments. Many were made from herbs such as rosemary, sage and fennel. Other natural remedies included garlic, mustard and cabbage. Many of the remedies would have done little good, but some of them did have the power to heal.

garlic

sage

rosemary

Keeping Clean

tepidarium (warm room)

THE ROMANS may not have all enjoyed good health, but they did like to keep clean. There were public toilets, flushed with constantly flowing water, and people regularly visited public baths. Most towns, even military bases on the frontiers of the Empire, had public bath houses.

The baths were more than just places to wash in. Bathers would meet their friends and spend the afternoon gossiping, in between dips in the bathing pools. Others would exercise, play ball games, or just relax. Businessmen even held meetings at the baths. Men and women used separate rooms or visited the bath house at different times. Slaves would bring bath towels and wooden-soled sandals. Bathers needed the sandals because many of the rooms had hot floors heated by a system of underfloor heating.

OIL FLASK AND STRIGILS
Romans used olive oil instead of soap. They would rub themselves with oil and scrape it off with a curved metal tool called a strigil. The oil would be kept in a small flask, like this one, which has two strigils chained to it.

warm air ducts in walls

BATHING AT BATH
This is a view of the Roman baths in the town of Bath, in Britain. The Romans built the baths there because of the natural hot spring, which bubbled up from the rocks at temperatures of up to 50°C. Rich in health-giving minerals, it attracted visitors from far and wide. This large lead-lined pool was used for swimming. In Roman times, it was covered by a roof.

frigidarium (cold room)

caldarium (hot room)

hot air from furnace

furnace

BATH HOUSE DIG

An archaeological dig in Britain has uncovered these remains of the foundations of a bath house. You can see the bottoms of the pillars that once supported the floor. Hot air from a furnace would have flowed around these pillars, heating the floor and the rooms above it.

THE BATHS

The public baths included exercise areas, changing rooms, a sauna and various pools. The rooms and water were heated by hot air from one or more underground furnaces. The *frigidarium*, or cold room, usually had an unheated pool for bathers to take an icy plunge and was often partly open-air. It led on to a warmer area, the *tepidarium*. In the warmth, bathers would rub themselves with oil, then scrape off any dirt or grime. When they were clean, they were ready to take a dip in the pool. The steamy *caldarium*, or hot room, was nearest to a furnace. Here, bathers could soak or sweat to their hearts' content.

PUBLIC TOILETS

The remains of public toilets like these have been found in many parts of the Empire. People used sponges on sticks to clean themselves. They could rinse the sponges in a channel of flowing water in front of them. Another channel of water, under the stone seats, carried away the waste.

103

Sport and Combat

MOST ROMANS preferred watching sport rather than taking part themselves. There were some, however, who enjoyed athletics and keeping fit. They took their exercise at the public baths and at the sports ground or *palaestra*. Men would compete at wrestling, long jump and swimming. Women would work out with weights.

Boxing matches and chariot races were always well attended. The races took place on a long, oval racetrack, called a circus. The crowds would watch with such excitement that violent riots often followed. Charioteers and their teams became big stars. Roman crowds also enjoyed watching displays of cruelty. Bloody battles between gladiators and fights among wild animals took place in a special oval arena, called an amphitheatre. Roman entertainments became more spectacular and bloodthirsty as time passed. They would even flood the arenas of amphitheatres for mock sea battles.

A COLOSSEUM
This is the colosseum in the Roman city of El Djem, in Tunisia. A colosseum was a kind of amphitheatre. Arenas such as this were built all over the Empire. The largest and most famous is the Colosseum in Rome.

DEATH OR MERCY?
Gladiators usually fought to the death, but a wounded gladiator could appeal for mercy. The excited crowd would look for the emperor's signal. A thumbs-up meant his life was spared. A thumbs-down meant he must die.

COME ON YOU REDS!

Charioteers belonged to teams and wore their team's colours when they raced. Some also wore protective leather helmets, like the one in this mosaic. In Rome, there were four teams – the Reds, Blues, Whites and Greens. Each team had faithful fans and charioteers were every bit as popular as football stars today.

A DAY AT THE RACES

This terracotta carving records an exciting moment at the races. Chariot racing was a passion for most Romans. Chariots were usually pulled by four horses, though just two or as many as six could be used. Accidents and foul play were common as the chariots thundered round the track.

THE CHAMP

Boxing was a deadly sport. Fighters, like this boxer, wore studded thongs instead of padded boxing gloves. Severe injuries, and even brain damage, were probably quite common.

THE GREEK IDEAL

The Romans admired all things Greek, including their love of athletics. This painted Greek vase dates from about 333BC and shows long-distance runners. However, Roman crowds were not interested in athletic contests in the Greek style, such as the Olympic Games.

Drama and Music

MUSIC AND SONGS were an important part of Roman life. Music was played at banquets, at weddings and funerals, at the theatre, in the home, at fights between gladiators and other public events. The Romans played a variety of musical instruments, including double flutes, pan pipes, lyres, cymbals, rattles and tambourines. These had already been well known in either Egypt or Greece. The Romans also had trumpets and horns, and water-powered organs.

Going to the theatre was a popular Roman pastime. The whole idea of drama came from Greece, so Greek comedies and tragedies were often performed. Roman writers produced plays in a similar style, as well as comic sketches and dances. The stage used the stone front of a building as a backdrop. Rising banks of stone or wooden seats curved around it in a half circle.

THE ENTERTAINERS
This mosaic from Pompeii shows a group of actors in a scene from a Greek play. Actors were always men, playing the parts of women whenever necessary. The role of actors in a play was shown by the colours of their costume and their masks. The piper in this mosaic is wearing the white mask of a female character.

MUSIC LESSONS
Girls from wealthy families often had music lessons at home. This wall painting shows a girl being taught to play the cithara, a type of lyre. The Romans adopted this harp-like instrument from the Greeks.

MAKE A MASK

You will need: self-drying clay, wooden board, rolling pin, large bowl, modelling knife, acrylic paints, paintbrush, water pot, scissors, cord, pencil, green paper or card, gardening wire, some coloured beads.

1 Put the clay on the board. Roll it out into a sheet that is bigger than the bowl you are using. Drape it over the bowl and shape it, as shown above.

2 Trim off the edges and cut out eye holes and a mouth. Roll out the clay you trimmed off and cut out a mouth and nose piece, as shown above. Make a small ball of clay, too.

3 Mould the nose on to the mask. Press the small ball of clay into the chin and put the mouth piece over it, as shown. Make a hole on each side of the mask, for the cord.

MUSICIANS
Some of the musicians in this procession are playing the *cornu*, a large curved horn. It was played at religious festivals and funerals, at public games, and by the Roman army.

ACTORS' MASKS
Roman actors wore masks and wigs to show the type of character they were playing. This detail of a mosaic from Rome shows the kind of elaborate masks they wore.

DRAMA IN THE OPEN AIR
Roman theatres were usually open to the sky. These are the ruins of the larger of the two theatres in Pompeii. It could seat up to 50,000 people. It had no roof, but could be covered by an awning to protect the audience from the hot summer sun.

4 When the clay is dry, paint the mask in bright colours. You can paint it like this one, shown above, or you could make up your own design. Leave the paint to dry.

5 Cut two lengths of cord. Thread them through the holes in the side of the mask, as shown. Secure with a knot. Tie the cord around your head when you wear the mask.

6 Draw, cut out and paint some leaf shapes. Thread them on to a length of wire, as shown. Thread beads between some of the leaves. Wind the wire round the top of the mask.

Actors' masks had large mouths for them to speak through. The actual masks were probably made of shaped and stiffened linen.

Fun and Games

ROMAN CHILDREN played games such as hide-and-seek, marbles and hopscotch, which are still popular today. Young children played with dolls and little figures of people and animals. These were made of wood, clay or bronze. A child from a wealthy family might be given a child-size chariot, to be pulled along by a goat.

Roman men and women loved playing board games. There were simple games, similar to noughts-and-crosses, and more complicated games, rather like chess or draughts. In some games, players had to race toward the finish. A dice was thrown to decide how many squares they could move at a time. They played with counters made of bone, glass or clay.

The Romans were great gamblers. They would place bets on a chariot race or a cock-fight or on throwing dice. Gambling became such a problem that games of chance were officially banned – except during the winter festival of Saturnalia, when most rules were relaxed. However, the rattle of dice could still be heard in most taverns and public baths.

PLAYING KNUCKLEBONES

Two women play the popular game of knucklebones, or *astragali*. The idea was to throw the knucklebones in the air and catch as many of them as possible on the back of your hand. The number you caught was your score.

KNUCKLEBONES

Most Romans used the ankle bones of sheep to play knucklebones. These had six sides and were also used as dice – each side had a different value. Wealthy Romans might use knucklebones made of glass, bronze or onyx, like these.

MARBLES

Roman children played with these marbles many centuries ago. Two are glass and one is made of pottery. Marbles were either rolled together or on to marked gaming boards. They were also thrown into pottery vases. Nuts, such as hazelnuts and walnuts, were often used like marbles.

MAKE A ROMAN GAME

You will need: self-drying clay, rolling pin, chopping board, modelling knife, ruler, glass tiles for making mosaics, two beads (in the same colours as your tiles).

1 Roll out the clay and trim it to about 25cm square. Use the ruler and knife to mark out a grid, 8 squares across and down, leaving a border around the edge.

2 Decorate the border using the clay you trimmed off, as shown above. Leave to dry. Each player chooses a colour and has 16 tiles and a bead – this is the *dux* or leader.

3 Players take turns to put their tiles on any squares, two at a time. The dux is put on last. Players now take turns to move a tile one square forward, backward or sideways.

Just Rolling Along

Children from poor families had few toys and had to work from a young age. However, even poor children found time to play, and made do with whatever was at hand. This boy is rolling wheels in front of him as he runs.

Your Throw!

This mosaic from Roman North Africa shows three men playing dice games in a tavern. The Romans loved to gamble and would bet on anything, including the roll of the dice. Large amounts could be won or lost on the score when the dice stopped rolling!

Counters

These gaming counters are made of bone and ivory. As well as using quite plain, round ones, the Romans liked to use counters carved in intricate shapes. Here you can see a ram's head, a hare and a lobster. The large round counter has two women carved on it.

Dice

Dice games were played by the poor and the rich. These dice have survived over the centuries. The largest is made of greenstone, the next is made of rock crystal, and the smallest is agate. The silver dice in the form of squatting figures were probably used by wealthy Romans.

4 If you sandwich your opponent's tile between two of yours, it is captured and removed. You then get an extra go. The dux is captured in the same way as any tile.

5 The dux can also jump over a tile to an empty square, as shown. If your opponent's tile is then trapped between your dux and one of your tiles, it is captured.

During the game, you must move a tile or dux if it is possible to do so – even if it means being captured. The winner is the first player to capture all of the other player's tiles and dux.

Religions and Festivals

THE ROMANS believed in many different gods and goddesses. Some of them were the same as the gods of ancient Greece, but with different names. Jupiter, the sky god, was the most powerful of all. Venus was the goddess of love, Mars was the god of war, Ceres the god of the harvest, Saturn the god of farmers, and Mercury of merchants. Household gods protected the home. Splendid temples were built in honour of the gods. The Pantheon, in Rome, is the largest and most famous. Special festivals for the gods were held during the year, with processions, music, offerings and animal sacrifices. The festivals were often public holidays. The mid-winter festival of Saturnalia, in honour of Saturn, lasted up to seven days.

As the Empire grew, many Romans adopted the religions of other peoples, such as the Egyptians and the Persians.

JUPITER
Jupiter was the chief god of the Romans. He was the all-powerful god of the sky. The Romans believed he showed his anger by hurling a thunderbolt to the ground.

THE PANTHEON
The Pantheon in Rome was a temple to all the gods. It was built between AD118 and 128. Its mosaic floor, interior columns and high dome still remain exactly as they were built.

DIANA THE HUNTRESS
Diana was the goddess of hunting and the Moon. In this detail from a floor mosaic, she is shown poised with a bow and arrow, ready for the hunt. Roman gods were often the same as the Greek ones, but were given different names. Diana's Greek name was Artemis.

A TEMPLE TO THE GODS

You will need: thick stiff card, thin card, old newspaper, scissors, balloon, PVA glue, ruler, pencils, masking tape, drinking straws, acrylic paints, paintbrush, water pot, Plasticine.

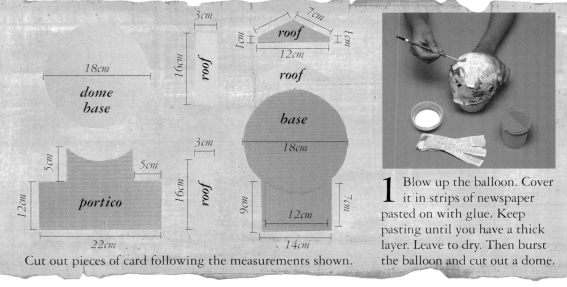

dome base — 18cm

roof — 3cm, 16cm

roof — 7cm, 1cm, 1cm, 12cm

portico — 5cm, 5cm, 12cm, 22cm

roof — 3cm, 16cm

base — 18cm, 9cm, 12cm, 7cm, 14cm

Cut out pieces of card following the measurements shown.

1 Blow up the balloon. Cover it in strips of newspaper pasted on with glue. Keep pasting until you have a thick layer. Leave to dry. Then burst the balloon and cut out a dome.

PRIESTS OF ISIS

The Egyptian mother-goddess Isis had many followers throughout the Roman Empire. This painting shows priests and worshippers of Isis taking part in a water purification ceremony. The ceremony would have been performed every afternoon.

BLESS THIS HOUSE

This is a bronze statue of a *lar* or household god. Originally gods of the countryside, the *lares* were believed to look after the family and the home. Every Roman home had a shrine to the *lares*. The family, including the children, would make daily offerings to the gods.

MITHRAS THE BULL-SLAYER

Mithras was the Persian god of light. He is shown here, in a marble relief from a temple, slaying a bull. This bull's blood was believed to have brought life to the Earth. The cult of Mithras spread through the whole Empire, and was particularly popular with Roman soldiers. However, only men were allowed to worship Mithras.

The Pantheon was built of brick and then clad in stone and marble. Its huge dome, with a diameter of over 43m, was the largest ever constructed until the 1900s.

2 Put the dome on its card base and draw its outline. Cut out the centre of the base to make a halo shape. Make a hole in the top of the dome. Bind the pieces together, as shown.

3 Glue together the base pieces. Cut a piece of thin card long enough to go round the base circle. This will be the circular wall. Use masking tape to hold the portico in shape.

4 Cut some straws into eight pieces, each 6cm long. These will be the columns for the entrance colonnade. Glue together the roof for the entrance. Secure with tape.

5 Glue together the larger pieces, as shown. Position each straw column with a small piece of Plasticine at its base. Glue on the entrance roof. Paint your model.

Family Occasions

THE FAMILY was very important to Romans. The father was the all-powerful head of the family, which included everyone in the household – wife, children, slaves, and even close relatives. In the early days of Rome, a father had the power of life and death over his children! However, Roman fathers were rarely harsh and children were much loved by both parents.

Childhood was fairly short. Parents would arrange for a girl to be betrothed at the age of 12, and a boy at 14. Marriages took place a few years later. Brides usually wore a white dress and a yellow cloak, with an orange veil and a wreath of sweetly-scented flowers. A sacrifice would be made to the gods, and everyone would wish the couple well. That evening, a procession with flaming torches and flute music would lead the newly-weds to their home.

Funerals were also marked with music and processions. By Roman law, burials and cremations had to take place outside the city walls.

HAPPY FAMILIES
This Roman tombstone from Germany shows a family gathered together for a meal. From the Latin inscription on it, we know that it was put up by a soldier of the legions, in memory of his dead wife. He lovingly describes her as the "sweetest and purest" of women.

D·M·C·IVL·MATERNVS
VET·EX·LEG·I·M·VIVS·SIBI
ET·MARIE·MARCELLINAE
COIIVGI·DVLCISSIME
CASTISSIME·OBITAE·F

MOTHER AND BABY
A mother tenderly places her baby in the cradle. When children were born, they were laid at the feet of their father. If he accepted the child into the family, he would pick it up. In wealthy families, a birth was a great joy, but for poorer families it just meant another mouth to feed. Romans named a girl on the 8th day after the birth, and a boy on the 9th day. The child was given a *bulla*, a charm to ward off evil spirits.

TOGETHERNESS
When a couple were engaged, they would exchange gifts as a symbol of their devotion to each other. A ring like this one might have been given by a man to his future bride. The clasped hands symbolize marriage. Gold pendants with similar patterns were also popular.

MOURNING THE DEAD

A wealthy Roman has died and his family have gone into mourning. Laments are played on flutes as they prepare his body for the funeral procession. The Romans believed that the dead went to Hades, the Underworld, which lay beyond the river of the dead. A coin was placed in the corpse's mouth, to pay the ferryman. Food and drink for the journey was buried with the body.

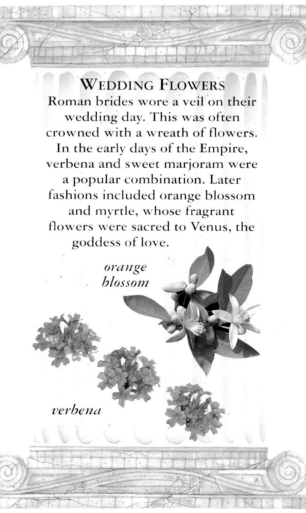

TILL DEATH US DO PART

A Roman marriage ceremony was rather like a present-day Christian wedding. The couple would exchange vows and clasp hands to symbolize their union. Here, the groom is holding the marriage contract, which would have been drawn up before the ceremony. Not everyone found happiness, however, and divorce was quite common.

WEDDING FLOWERS

Roman brides wore a veil on their wedding day. This was often crowned with a wreath of flowers. In the early days of the Empire, verbena and sweet marjoram were a popular combination. Later fashions included orange blossom and myrtle, whose fragrant flowers were sacred to Venus, the goddess of love.

orange blossom

verbena

Soldiers of the Legion

THE ARMY OF THE EARLY EMPIRE was divided into 28 groups called legions. Each of these numbered about 5,500 soldiers. The legion included mounted troops and foot-soldiers. They were organized into cohorts, of about 500 men, and centuries, of about 80 men – even though centuries means 'hundreds'. Each legion was led into battle by soldiers carrying standards. These were decorated poles that represented the honour and bravery of the legion.

The first Roman soldiers were called up from the wealthier families in times of war. These conscripts had to supply their own weapons. In later years, the Roman army became paid professionals, with legionaries recruited from all citizens. During the period of the Empire, many foreign troops also fought for Rome as auxiliary soldiers.

Army life was tough and discipline was severe. After a long march carrying heavy kits, tents, tools and weapons, the weary soldiers would have to dig camp defences. A sentry who deserted his post would be beaten to death.

AT WAR
Trajan's Column in Rome is decorated with scenes from the Dacian wars. These were fought in the region of present-day Romania. Scenes like these can tell us much about Roman soldiers, the weapons they used, their enemies and their allies.

A LEGIONARY
This bronze statue of a legionary is about 1,800 years old. He is wearing a crested parade helmet and the overlapping bronze armour of the period. Legionaries underwent strict training and were brutally disciplined. They were tough soldiers and quite a force to be reckoned with.

ON HORSEBACK
Roman foot-soldiers were backed up by mounted troops, or cavalry. They were divided into groups, of 500 to 1,000, called *alae*. The cavalry were amongst the highest paid of Roman soldiers.

RAISING THE STANDARD

The Emperor Constantine addresses his troops, probably congratulating them on a victory. They are carrying standards, emblems of each legion. Standards were decorated with gold eagles, hands, wreaths and banners called *vexilla*. They were symbols of the honour and bravery of the legion and had to be protected at all costs.

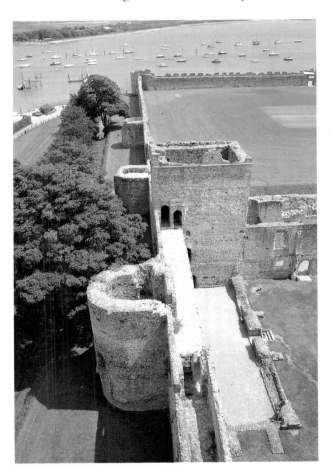

A ROMAN FORT

The Roman army built forts of wood or stone all over the Empire. This fort is in southern Britain. It was built to defend the coast against attacks by Saxon raiders from northern Europe. Today, its surrounding area is called Porchester. The name comes from a combination of the word port and *caster*, the Latin word for fort.

HADRIAN'S WALL

This is part of Hadrian's Wall, which marks the most northerly border of the Roman Empire. It stretches for 120km across northern England, almost from coast to coast. It was built as a defensive barrier between AD122 and 128, at the command of the Emperor Hadrian.

Weapons and Armour

ROMAN SOLDIERS were well equipped. A legionary was armed with a dagger, called a *pugio*, and a short iron sword, called a *gladius*, which was used for stabbing and slashing. He carried a javelin, or *pilum*, made of iron and wood. In the early days, a foot-soldier's armour was a mail shirt, worn over a short, thick tunic. Officers wore a cuirass, a bronze casing that protected the chest and back. By about AD35, the mail shirt was being replaced by plate armour made of iron. The metal sections were joined by hooks or by leather straps. Officers wore varying crests to show their rank. Early shields were oval, and later ones were oblong with curved edges. They were made of layers of wood glued together, covered in leather and linen. A metal boss, or cover, over the central handle could be used to hit an enemy who got too close.

HEAD GEAR
Helmets were designed to protect the sides of the head and the neck. This cavalry helmet is made of bronze and iron. It would have been worn by an auxiliary, a foreign soldier fighting for Rome sometime after AD43. Officers wore crests on their helmets, so that their men could see them during battle.

ROMAN SOLDIERS
Artists over the ages have been inspired by the battles of the Roman legions. They imagined how fully armed Roman soldiers might have looked. This picture shows a young officer giving orders.

ROMAN ARMOUR

You will need: tape measure, A1-size sheets of silver card (one or two, depending on how big you are), scissors, pencil, PVA glue, paintbrush, 2m length of cord, compass.

1 Measure yourself around your chest. Cut out three strips of card, 5cm wide and long enough to go round you. Cut out some thinner strips to stick these three together.

2 Lay the wide strips flat and glue them together with the thin strips, as shown above. The Romans would have used leather straps to hold the wide metal pieces together.

3 When the glue is dry, bend the ends together, silver side out. Make a hole in the end of each strip and thread the cord through, as shown above.

TORTOISE TACTICS

Siege tactics were one of the Roman army's great strengths. When approaching an enemy fortress, a group of soldiers could lock their shields together over their heads and crouch under them. Protected by their shields, they could safely advance toward the enemy. This was known as the tortoise, or *testudo*, formation. During a siege, catapults were used to hurl iron bolts and large stones over fortress walls.

DEADLY WEAPONS

These iron spearheads were found on the site of an old Roman fort near Bath, in Britain. The wooden shafts they were on rotted long ago. Roman soldiers carried both light and heavy spears. The lighter ones were used for throwing, and the heavier ones were for thrusting at close range.

SWORDS

Both short and long swords would have been kept in a scabbard. This spectacular scabbard was owned by an officer who served the Emperor Tiberius. It may have been given to him by the emperor himself. It is elaborately decorated in gold and silver.

Put the shoulder piece over your head and tie the chest section round yourself. Now you are a legionary ready to do battle with the enemies of Rome. Metal strip armour was invented during the reign of the Emperor Tiberius, AD14-37. Originally, the various parts were hinged and were joined together either by hooks or by buckles and straps.

4 Cut a square of card as wide as your shoulders. Use the compass to draw a 12cm diameter circle in the centre. Cut the square in half and cut away the half circles.

5 Use smaller strips of card to glue the shoulder halves together, leaving a neck hole. Cut out four more strips, two a little shorter than the others. Attach them in the same way.

Ships and Sailors

THE ROMANS USED SHIPS for trade, transport and warfare. Roman warships were slim, fast vessels called galleys. They were powered by oarsmen who sat below deck. A standard Roman war galley had 270 oarsmen. It also had a large, square sail that was used for more speed when the wind was favourable.

All kinds of goods, from wool and pottery to marble and grain, had to be moved around the Empire. Most goods, especially heavy cargoes of food or building materials, were moved by water. Merchant ships were deeper, heavier and slower than galleys. They had big, flapping sails and longer oars to make steering easier. Barges were used on rivers.

CONTAINERS
Oil and wine were often shipped in large pottery jars called *amphorae*. Here, an amphora is being carried from one ship to another. The amphorae were usually stacked in the ship's hold, with layers of brushwood as padding.

AT THE DOCKS
This wall painting from the port of Ostia shows a merchant ship being loaded. Heavy sacks of grain are being carried on board. You can see the two large steering oars at the stern, or rear, of the ship.

The Romans built lighthouses on treacherous coasts – stone towers topped by big lanterns or blazing beacons. Pirates, uncharted waters and the weather also made sea travel dangerous.

ROLLING ON THE RIVER
Wine and other liquids were sometimes stored in barrels. These were transported by river barges, like the one in this carving. Barrels of wine would be hauled from the vineyards of Germany or southern France to the nearest seaport.

MAKE AN AMPHORA
You will need: large sheet of thin card, ruler, two pencils, scissors, corrugated cardboard – two circles of 10cm and 20cm in diameter, two strips of 40cm x 30cm and another large piece, masking tape, PVA glue, old newspaper, paintbrush, reddish-brown acrylic paint, water pot.

1 Cut two pieces of card – 5cm and 38cm in depth. Tape the short piece to the small circle. Curl the long piece to make the neck. Make two holes in the side and tape it to the large circle.

2 Roll up the strips of corrugated cardboard. Bend them, as shown, fitting one end to the hole in the neck and the other to the cardboard. Fix in place with glue and tape.

3 Cut a piece of card, 40cm square. Roll it into a cylinder shape. Cut four lines, 10cm long, at one end, so it can be tapered into a point, as shown. Bind with tape.

SAILING OFF TO BATTLE

This painting imagines the impressive spectacle of a Roman war galley leaving harbour on its way to battle. Galleys were powered by rows of oarsmen, who sat on benches below deck. The helmsman, who controlled the galley's steering, shouted orders down to them. This galley has three banks, or layers, of oars. An underwater battering ram stuck out from the bow, or front, of war galleys. During a sea battle, the mast was lowered and the galley would try to ram the enemy ship. With the ram stuck in its side, Roman soldiers could easily board the enemy ship to finish the fight man to man.

An amphora like this one might have been used to carry wine, oil or fish sauce. Its long, pointed end would be stuck into layers of brushwood for support during transport.

4 To give the amphora a more solid base, roll up a cone of corrugated cardboard and stick it around the tapered end. Push a pencil into the end, as shown. Tape in position.

5 Stick the neck on to the main body. Cover the whole piece with strips of newspaper brushed on with glue. Leave to dry. Repeat until you have built up a thick layer.

6 When the paper is dry, paint the amphora. Roman amphorae were made of clay, so use a reddish-brown paint to make yours look like it is clay. Leave to dry.

Builders of the Empire

THE ROMANS were great builders and engineers. As the legions conquered foreign lands, they built new roads to carry their supplies and messengers. The roads were very straight, stretching across hundreds of kilometres. They were built with a slight hump in the middle so that rainwater drained off to the sides. Some were paved with stone and others were covered with gravel or stone chippings. Roman engineers also used their skills to bring water supplies to their cities by building aqueducts.

The Romans constructed great domes, arched bridges and grand public buildings all across the Empire. Local supplies of stone and timber were used. Stone was an important Roman building material, but had to be quarried and transported to sites. The Romans were the first to develop concrete, which was cheaper and stronger than stone.

The rule of the Romans came to an end in western Europe over 1,500 years ago. Yet reminders of their skills and organization are still visible today.

ROMAN ROADS
A typical Roman road, stretching into the distance as far as the eye can see. It runs through the coastal town of Ostia, in Italy. It was the 1800s before anyone in Europe could build roads to match those of ancient Rome.

MUSCLE POWER
This stone carving shows how Romans used big wooden cranes to lift heavy building materials. The crane is powered by a huge treadwheel. Slaves walk round and round in the wheel, making it turn. The turning wheel pulls on the rope, that is tied round the heavy block of stone, raising it off the ground.

MAKE A GROMA
You will need: large, strong piece of cardboard, scissors, ruler, pencil, square of card, PVA glue, masking tape, balsa wood pole, Plasticine, silver foil, string, large sewing needle, acrylic paints, paintbrush, water pot, broom handle.

1 Cut out three pieces of cardboard – two 20cm x 6cm, one 40cm x 6cm. Cut another piece, 15cm x 12cm, for the handle. Then cut them into shape, as shown above.

2 Measure to the centre of the long piece. Use a pencil to make a slot here, between the layers of cardboard. The slot is for the balsa wood pole.

3 Slide the balsa wood pole into the slot and tape the cardboard pieces in a cross. Use the card square to make sure the four arms of the groma are at right angles. Glue in place.

BUILDING MATERIALS

The Romans used a variety of stones for building. Local quarries were the most common source. Limestone and a volcanic rock called tufa were used in Pompeii. Slate was used for roofing in parts of Britain. Fine marble, used for temples and other public buildings, was available in the Carrara region of Italy, as it still is today. However, it was also imported from overseas.

marble

slate

SURVIVING THE CENTURIES

This Roman bridge crosses the River Guadalquivir at Cordoba in Spain. The Romans had no bulldozers or power tools, and yet their buildings and monuments have survived thousands of years.

WALLS OF ROME

The city of Rome's defences were built at many stages in its history. These sturdy walls were raised during the reign of the Emperor Marcus Aurelius, AD121–180. Known as the Aurelian Walls, they are still in good condition today.

Slot the arms on to the balsa wood pole. Use the plumb lines as a guide to make sure the pole is vertical. The arms can then be used to line up objects in the distance. Romans used a groma to measure right angles and to make sure roads were straight.

4 Roll the Plasticine into four small cones and cover them with foil. Thread string through the tops, as shown. These are the groma's plumb lines, or vertical guides.

5 Tie the plumb lines to each arm, as shown. They must all hang at the same length – 20cm will do. If the Plasticine is too heavy, use wet newspaper rolled up in the foil.

6 Split the top of the handle piece, and wrap it round the balsa wood pole. Glue it in place, as shown. Do the same on the other end with the broom handle. Paint the groma.

GLOSSARY

A

Acropolis A sacred hill overlooking Athens on which temples were built.

agora A market-place in ancient Greece.

amphitheatre An oval open-air arena surrounded by seats.

amphora (plural: amphorae) A pottery storage jar, often shaped like a tall vase with handles and a pointed base.

anvil A block used by smiths for shaping hot metals.

aqueduct An artificial channel for carrying water.

Archimedes screw A device for lifting water from one level to another, named after its inventor, the Greek scientist Archimedes.

arena The sand floor area in an amphitheatre.

atrium The hallway or courtyard in a Roman house. The centre of the atrium was open to the sky.

auloi A pair of musical pipes in ancient Greece.

B

basilica A huge building in the forum of a Roman city. It was a cross between a town hall and law courts.

brazier A bronze container filled with hot coals, used for heating rooms.

bronze A metal made by mixing tin with copper. Bronze was used for making armour.

C

catapult A large wooden structure used to fire stones and iron bolts at the enemy.

centaur A mythical beast, half man, half horse.

century A unit of the Roman army, numbering from 80 to 100 soldiers.

chariot A lightweight cart drawn by horses.

circus An oval track used for chariot races.

city-state A centre of government. Ancient Greece was made up of about 300 city-states.

civilization A society that has made advances in the arts, science and technology, law or government.

cohort A division of the Roman army, at times numbering about 500 soldiers.

consul One of the two leaders of the Roman republic, elected each year.

cosmology The study of the workings of the universe.

cuirass Armour that protects the upper part of the body.

curia The council in ancient Roman cities.

D

Delphi The place the Greeks believed to be the centre of the world.

democracy A system of government by the many.

E

electrum A mixture of gold and silver, used for making coins.

empire A large number of different lands ruled over by a single person or government.

F

flax A plant with stems used to make linen.

forceps Surgical instruments shaped like pincers or tongs.

forum The town centre or downtown area of a Roman city.

fresco A painting applied to damp plaster and used to decorate walls in the homes of wealthy people.

G

galley A warship powered by oars.

gladiator A professional fighter, a slave or a criminal who fought to the death for public entertainment.

gorgon A Greek female monster of such horrific appearance that anyone who looked at her was turned to stone.

greaves Armour for the legs.

grid pattern A criss-cross pattern of straight lines at right angles. It was used to divide a town into blocks and straight streets.

groma An instrument used by Roman surveyors. They used it to measure right angles and to make sure roads were straight.

gruel A soup of cereal and water, such as porridge.

guild A society that protected the interests of people working within a trade.

H

helot A slave in Sparta.

J

javelin A throwing spear.

K

kiln An industrial oven, or a furnace.

kindling Twigs, woodchips or other material used to start a fire.

knucklebones A favourite game of the Greeks. It involved flipping small animal bones from one side of the hand to the other without dropping them.

L

legion A section of the Roman army made up only of Roman citizens.

lekythoi White clay flasks used at Greek funerals.

Linear A A script used by the Minoans.

litter A form of transport in which a seat or platform is carried by bearers.

lyre One of various harp-like instruments played in ancient Greece and Rome.

M

mail Chain armour, made up of interlocking iron rings.

metic A foreigner resident in Athens.

metronomoi Athenian officials whose job it was to stop merchants and traders from cheating one another.

Minoan The first great Greek civilization.

Minotaur A mythical beast, half man, half bull.

mosaic A picture or patterned floor made up of coloured pebbles or small squares of glass, stone or pottery.

Mount Olympus Home of the Greek gods and goddesses.

myrrh A kind of resin from shrubs, used to make perfume and medicine.

mythology Traditional stories about the exploits of gods and legendary heroes.

O

ochre A kind of yellow or reddish-coloured earth.

oligarchy Government by a group of rich and powerful people.

Olympic Games A sporting competition held every four years at Olympia in honour of the god Zeus. The first Games were held in 776BC.

Oracle A spirit that could see into the future.

P

palla A veil worn over the head or shoulders by Roman women.

Panathenaic festival A yearly procession with sacrifices in honour of Athena.

pankration A gruesome fighting sport that combined boxing and wrestling.

papyrus A tall reed that grows in the River Nile, used to make a kind of paper.

Parthenon A temple on the Acropolis in Athens dedicated to the city's goddess, Athena.

patrician A member of one of the old, wealthy and powerful families in ancient Rome.

pectoral Jewellery or armour worn on the breast or chest.

peplos A robe presented to the goddess Athena once every four years at the Panathenaic festival.

phalanx A solid block of foot soldiers in battle.

philosophy A Greek word meaning love of knowledge.

plate armour Fitted body armour made of linked sheets of solid metal.

plebeian A member of the (free) common people of ancient Rome.

priest Someone who offered prayers and sacrifices on behalf of worshippers at a temple.

Propylaea The momumental gateways to the temple

complex on top of the Acropolis, Athens.

Pythia The priestess who officiated at Delphi.

pyxis A box used in ancient Greece for storing face powder or other cosmetics.

R

ram A large, pointed beam extending from the hull, or front, of an ancient warship. It was used to ram into the side of an enemy ship.

republic A state that is governed by an assembly of its citizens rather than by a king.

S

Samian ware A type of glazed, red-clay pottery that was popular throughout the Roman Empire.

Saturnalia A winter festival held in honour of the god Saturn.

Senate The law-making assembly of ancient Rome.

slaves People who were not free, but owned by their masters.

stola A long dress worn by Roman women over a tunic.

strigil A metal scraper used for cleaning the body.

stylus A pointed tool, such as the one used to scratch words on to a wax tablet.

T

tablinium The formal reception room and study in a Roman house.

terracotta A mixture of baked clay and sand used to make statues, figurines and pottery.

toga A white woollen robe.

tortoise or testudo A method of covering a group of soldiers with shields to protect them.

treadwheel A wooden wheel turned by the feet of people, used to power mills or other machinery.

triclinium Dining room. Its name comes from the Roman tradition of having an arrangement of three (tri)

couches to lie on while dining.

trident A three-pronged spear used by fishermen and gladiators.

tunic A loose robe worn as everyday clothing by men and women.

U

Underworld A mysterious place to which the spirits of the dead were believed to travel after burial.

V

villa A Roman country house, often decorated with mosaics and wall paintings. Villas were usually part of an agricultural estate.

W

water clock A bucket full of water with a hole in the bottom. The flow of water worked a dial, which told the time.

wet nurse A woman employed to breastfeed babies.

Index

headdresses 88–9
heating 102–103
Hephaestus 24, 25
Hera 41, 44, 54, 55
Heracles 41, 44, 46
Herculaneum 66, 70, 79
Hermes 40, 45
heroes 44–5, 48, 62
Hestia 28
hieroglyphs 10, 16
Hippocrates 58
Homer 4, 13, 14, 44, 62
homes 28–9
hoplites 60, 61, 62
horses 60, 61
houses 76, 78, 80–1
hunting 30, 77, 98, 110
Hygieia 35, 100

I
inscriptions 66, 91, 112
Isis 111

J
jewellery 18, 38, 39, 52,
   53, 67, 88–9, 112
Julius Caesar 69–72
Jupiter 6, 67, 110

K
keys 80
kitchens 82–4
Knossos 11, 16
knucklebones 34–5

L
lamps 94
Latin 6, 66, 68, 74,
   88, 90–1, 96, 112
laws 20, 21
legions 114–15, 120
leg offering 58–9
Leonidas, King 26, 27
Lycurgus 27

M
Macedonia 12, 14, 53
make-up 88
markets 92–4
marriage 112–13
masks 19, 48–9, 106–7
mathematics 10, 56, 57
medicine 10, 58–9, 100–1
Mediterranean Sea 67, 78
Medusa 44–5
metalwork 96
metics 22, 23
Minoans 4, 10, 11, 12,
   16–17
Minotaur 44
Mithras 111
money 67–8, 75, 93–4, 113
mosaics 76–7, 80, 98–9,
   105–6, 109–10

Muses 52
music 43, 50–1, 85, 90,
   99, 106–7, 110,
   112–13
Mycenaeans 4, 10, 11, 12,
   18–19
myths 44–5

N
Nero, Emperor 71

O
Odysseus 13, 34, 45
olive oil 77, 82, 102
Olympic Games 4, 12,
   54, 55
Olympus, Mount 40, 46
omphalos 11
open-air theatres 6
Orpheus 50
Ostia 66, 95, 118, 120
ostracism 25
oxen 30, 31

P
paintings 85–6, 88–90,
   98–9
palaces 17
pancakes with honey 32–3
Pantheon 70, 110–11
Parthenon 4, 10, 13, 24,
   40–3
patricians 74
Pegasus 45
Peloponnesian Wars 12, 14
Penelope 34
Pericles 14, 15, 20
Persephone 47
Perseus 45
Persian Wars 12, 13, 15,
   24, 27, 63

philosophy 6, 10, 56
plebeians 67, 74
politics 20–1, 56
Pompeii 6, 7, 66, 70,
   78–9, 86, 90, 92, 98–9,
   106–7, 121
Poseidon 30, 43
pottery 11, 16, 18, 22, 30,
   53, 62, 85, 94, 96–8,
   108, 118
Praetorian Guards 73
priests 40, 42, 54, 72, 111
processions 72, 110,
   112–13

R
religion 40–2, 50, 54,
   72, 110
republic 67, 72
Rhodes 53
roads 67, 70, 78, 120
Roman Empire 6–7, 12, 15
Romulus 5, 66, 70, 72

S
sacrifices 25, 29, 31, 35
sandals 86, 102
Sappho 14
Saturnalia 108, 110
Schliemann, Heinrich 19
science 6–7
scrolls 36–7
seal, Minoan 16–17
Senate 69, 72, 74